Simply Delicious

The majority of the recipes in this book
were previously published in *The Complete
Bocuse* © Flammarion, S.A., Paris, 2012

Photography by Jean-Charles Vaillant
Food Styling by Éric Trochon

Translated from the French
by Carmella Abramowitz-Moreau
Additional translation (pp. 151 and 213):
Anne McDowall
Design: Alice Leroy
Typesetting: Claude-Olivier Four
Color separation: IGS-CP, Paris
Printed in Spain by Macrolibros

Simultaneously published in French as *Paul Bocuse,
Mes meilleures recettes simples et gourmandes*
© Flammarion, S.A., Paris, 2014

English-language edition
© Flammarion, S.A., Paris, 2014

editions.flammarion.com

14 15 16 3 2 1

ISBN: 978-2-08-020203-1

Dépôt légal: 05/2014

Paul Bocuse

Simply Delicious

Flammarion

Contents

Contents

183 | Desserts

224 | Appendixes

Soup

SERVES 4
PREPARATION TIME: 10 MINUTES
COOKING TIME: 35 MINUTES

Leek and Potato Soup
Soupe poireaux-pommes de terre

1 lb. (500 g) potatoes

4 medium leeks

6 cups (1.5 liter) water

1 ½ teaspoons (10 g) kosher salt

2 tablespoons (30 g) butter

6 tablespoons (100 ml) crème fraîche or heavy cream

Pepper

Pork rind (optional)

In a large saucepan, bring the water and salt to a boil.

Peel, wash, and dice the potatoes. Peel and carefully wash the leeks, and dice them using scissors.

In another large saucepan, melt the butter, add the leeks and cook over low heat until they have softened completely. Pour in the boiling water, add the potatoes, and cook uncovered over moderate heat for 20 minutes, then stir in the cream, add a little pepper, cook for 5 minutes more, and serve.

Variation: In Lyon, a version of this soup is made using a local preparation called *couennes cuites en paquets*–"pork rind cooked in packets." You can make something similar by buying large pieces of fresh pork rind and cutting them into strips about 16 in. (40 cm) long and 2 in. (5 cm) wide. Fold each piece in four, like an accordion, and tie kitchen string tightly around the middle; the result will be the size and shape of a bow tie (in fact, in Lyon, bow ties are called *paquets de couennes*). Add two of these "packets" to the soup 10 minutes before it has finished cooking. Serve them in a separate bowl with a little of the soup to keep them warm, and eat them with black olives and mustard (if making the soup this way, don't add the cream).

Note: The pork rind that can be bought in Lyon is fresh but pre-cooked. Since this may not be readily available elsewhere, simply place pork rind in cold water, bring to a boil, and poach for 1½ hours. Allow it to cool before cutting, tying, and cooking it in the soup as described above (when tying, be careful not to allow the string to cut the rind).

SERVES 4
PREPARATION TIME: 20 MINUTES
COOKING TIME: 35 MINUTES

1 ½ lb. (700 g) winter squash

2 medium potatoes (about 10 oz./300g), peeled and diced

2 medium leeks

6 cups (1.5 liter) cold water

1 ½ teaspoons (10 g) kosher salt

4 tablespoons (60 g) butter, plus butter for browning the croutons

Salt and pepper

12 slices French bread, or 4 slices ordinary bread cut into quarters

6 tablespoons (100 ml) crème fraîche or heavy cream

Nutmeg

Winter Squash Soup
Soupe de courge

Peel and seed the winter squash, rinse it under cold water, and cut into cubes of roughly 1 in. (2 cm). Peel, rinse, and dice the potatoes. Clean and slice the leeks.

Place the winter squash and potatoes in a large saucepan with the water and salt, and bring to a boil. Meanwhile, melt the butter in a frying pan, add the leeks and cook slowly until they have melted down, then add them to the saucepan. Boil the soup over moderate heat, uncovered, for 20 minutes, then purée it in a blender, food processor, or by using a food mill. The result should be creamy; add salt and pepper and cook for 5 to 7 minutes more over low heat.

Brown the slices of bread in butter to make croutons, place them on a plate, and cover with a clean cloth to keep them warm.

Pour the cream into a warm soup tureen and stir in the soup little by little. Add a little nutmeg and serve with the croutons on the side.

Elysée Truffle Soup
Soupe aux truffes Elysée

SERVES 1
PREPARATION TIME: 20 MINUTES
COOKING TIME: 40 MINUTES

2 tablespoons of finely diced mixed carrots, onions, celery, and mushrooms in equal proportions

Butter for sautéing

2 oz. (50 g) fresh raw truffles

⅔ oz. (20 g) foie gras

1 cup (250 ml) chicken stock

2 ½ oz. (60 g) puff pastry

1 egg yolk

Special equipment: a small ovenproof soup dish, such as one you would use for a portion of onion soup

Sauté the diced vegetables gently in butter. Slice the truffle irregularly and cut the foie gras into differently sized pieces.

Preheat the oven to 425°F (220°C).

Place the sautéed vegetables in a soup bowl together with the truffle slices, pieces of foie gras, and the chicken stock.

Roll out the puff pastry very thinly and brush it with egg yolk. Fit it snugly over the soup bowl so that the contents are airtight.

Place the soup bowl in the oven. It will cook fairly quickly. The puff pastry will rise and turn a lovely golden color when it is done.

To enjoy this soup, break the puff pastry with a spoon so that the crumbs fall into the bowl.

This truffle soup was created specially for M. Valéry Giscard d'Estaing, former French president, and his wife, and served at a sumptuous dinner for the finest French cooks. It was at this reception that the President awarded me the Croix de la Légion d'Honneur, for my work as an ambassador of French cuisine, on Tuesday February 25, 1975.

SERVES 4
PREPARATION TIME: 20 MINUTES
COOKING TIME: 45 MINUTES

4 medium onions

4 tablespoons (60 g) butter, divided

2 tablespoons (12 g) flour

6 cups (1.5 liter) beef bouillon or water

1 loaf (250 g) of French bread

1 cup (100 g) freshly grated Gruyère cheese

Pepper

3 tablespoons (30 g) bread crumbs

Onion Soup
Soupe à l'oignon

Peel and slice the onions. Melt 2 tablespoons (30 g) of the butter in a large saucepan, add the onions, and brown lightly. Stir in the flour and, when it begins to color, add the bouillon or water, stirring constantly. Cook uncovered over moderate heat for 15 minutes.

Cut the bread in half lengthwise. Toast the bread under the broiler, then cut it into thick slices.

Preheat the oven to 350°F (180°C).

Place a third of the bread in an ovenproof soup tureen. Sprinkle it with a quarter of the grated cheese, 2 teaspoons of the remaining butter, softened, and a little pepper. Make three layers in this way, then pour the soup into the tureen, sprinkle with the bread crumbs and the remaining cheese, and place in the oven for 20 minutes or until the cheese and bread crumbs have browned. Serve immediately.

Variation: A richer soup can be made by beating three egg yolks in a bowl with a few spoonfuls of heavy cream, a little port, and a pinch of nutmeg. Whisk in a ladleful of the soup and simmer (do not boil), stirring constantly until the mixture begins to thicken. Pour this mixture into the tureen over the bread and cheese, add the remaining soup, and finish as described above.

This soup is traditionally served to French party guests in the early morning hours but can be enjoyed at any meal.

Home-Style Vegetable Soup
Soupe bonne femme

SERVES 4
PREPARATION TIME: 15 MINUTES
COOKING TIME: 35 MINUTES

1 large onion, peeled

2 medium potatoes

1 large or 2 small leeks

About 9 oz. (250 g) young green cabbage

6 cups (1.5 liter) water

1 ½ teaspoons (10 g) kosher salt

7 tablespoons (100 g) butter, divided

2 cups tightly packed (100 g) sorrel leaves

Nutmeg

Salt and pepper

Bring the water and kosher salt to a boil in a large saucepan. Peel the onions and potatoes. Wash all the vegetables. Thinly slice the onion, leeks, and cabbage, and dice the potatoes. In another large saucepan, melt 5 tablespoons (70 g) of the butter; when it is sizzling hot, add the onions and leeks. Lightly brown the vegetables over moderate heat, then add the cabbage and stir until it has melted down. Pour the boiling water into the pot with the vegetables, add the potatoes, and simmer uncovered for 30 minutes. Chop then add the sorrel and cook for 5 minutes more.

Warm the soup tureen by pouring a little boiling water into it, swirling it around, and pouring it out.

Add a little nutmeg, salt, and pepper to taste, then pour the soup into the tureen. Stir the remaining 2 tablespoons (30 g) of butter into it and serve.

Crayfish Bisque
Bisque d'écrevisses

SERVES 8
PREPARATION TIME: 20 MINUTES
COOKING TIME: 35 MINUTES

20 crayfish, 1 ½ oz. (40 g) apiece

5 oz. (150 g) rice

4 cups (1 liter) white stock, veal or chicken, divided

1 ½ oz. (40 g) carrots

1 ½ oz. (40 g) onion

1 sprig thyme

¼ bay leaf

Scant ½ cup (100 ml) cognac

1 cup (200 ml) dry white wine

1 ⅓ sticks (5 oz./150 g) unsalted butter

Crème fraîche (optional)

Salt and pink peppercorns or piment d'Espelette

Carefully wash the rice and cook it in 3 cups (750 ml) of the stock. While it is cooking, chop the carrot and onion into very fine dice (a mirepoix). Gently melt a knob of butter in a sauté pan and sweat the diced vegetables, ensuring they do not color. Add the thyme and bay leaf. Increase the heat to maximum and add the crayfish to the aromatic base. Season with salt and pepper. Sauté the crayfish quickly–they will immediately turn red. Pour over the cognac and flambé. As quickly as possible, pour over the white wine to extinguish the flames. Cook for 8 minutes.

Pour the sautéd mirepoix into a mortar or food processor. Using a few tablespoons of the stock, rinse out the pan and add this too.

Remove the flesh from the tails of half the crayfish. Place the crayfish flesh in a little stock and put the shells into a large mortar (or processor). Crush the shells into a fine paste. Drain the rice and incorporate the rice and the crayfish flesh to the crushed shells immediately. Crush the mixture again with the pestle, or process it, until the texture is creamy. Then strain it through a fine sieve, pressing all the liquid through until all that remains are the dried-out, powdered shells.

Return the mixture to a pot and bring to a brisk boil. Dilute the creamed crayfish with white stock or crème fraîche until the consistency is right. Remove from the heat and incorporate the remaining butter. Season lightly with the red peppercorns or piment d'Espelette.

To serve, slice the whole crayfish tails and garnish the soup with them. When it is ready, this soup should be the same red as the cooked crayfish.

Appetizers

SERVES 4
PREPARATION TIME: 15 MINUTES

10 oz. (300 g) medium-sized firm white button mushrooms

1 pinch sugar

Juice of 1 lemon

1 tablespoon crème fraîche or oil

Aromatic herbs, such as tarragon, chervil, chopped fennel, thyme flowers, crushed garlic, or spices of your choice

Salt and freshly ground pepper

Mushroom Salad
Salade de champignons

Clean, wash, and carefully dry the mushrooms. Finely slice them and place them in a salad dish.

Season with salt and freshly ground pepper, sugar, lemon juice, and crème fraîche (or oil).

Season with herbs or spices of your choice and serve chilled.

SERVES 4

PREPARATION TIME: 15 MINUTES
COOKING TIME: 6 MINUTES
MARINATING TIME: 2 DAYS

1 small red cabbage or Savoy cabbage

1 clove garlic

½ bay leaf, broken into small pieces

1 ¾ cups (400 ml) white wine vinegar

3 tablespoons walnut oil

Table salt and freshly ground pepper

Red Cabbage or Savoy Cabbage Salad
Salade de chou rouge ou chou de Milan

Remove the outer leaves of the small cabbage and pick the inner leaves off. Trim the ribs, wash the leaves, and drain them. Arrange them in small piles to cut them into fine julienne strips. Prepare using either of the two methods given below.

First method

Boil the julienned cabbage for 6 minutes and drain thoroughly. Arrange the slices in a mixing bowl in layers; on top of each layer sprinkle a little table salt and freshly ground black pepper, and insert the garlic clove and ½ bay leaf. Bring the vinegar briefly to a boil and allow to cool. Pour the cooled vinegar over the cabbage so it is completely covered. Leave to marinate in an airtight container in the refrigerator for 2 days, checking periodically that the cabbage is well covered with the vinegar. When it is ready, you can use it:

    a) as it is;

    b) drained and seasoned with walnut oil, using 3 tablespoons per 5 oz. (150 g) cabbage;

    c) seasoned and combined with an equal weight of finely sliced tart apples.

Second method

Bring the vinegar to a boil in a saucepan. Add the julienned cabbage and bring to a brisk boil. Then leave to cool. Drain, but not thoroughly (leave some of the cooking liquid), and just before serving, season with salt, pepper, and oil.

Each of these methods softens the cabbage and makes it more easily digestible.

SERVES 4
PREPARATION TIME: 15 MINUTES
COOKING TIME: 30 TO
35 MINUTES

Quenelles au Gratin

4 large quenelles, either store-bought or homemade

3 tablespoons (40 g) butter

½ cup (40 g) grated Gruyère cheese

Salt and freshly ground pepper

A little grated nutmeg

Shelled shrimps (optional)

Buy or make your favorite quenelles: poultry, pike, etc.

Preheat the oven to 425°F (210°C).

Generously butter an ovenproof dish and arrange the quenelles in it. Bake for about 15 to 20 minutes, keeping a careful eye on them. About 15 minutes before the end of the cooking time, sprinkle the quenelles with the grated cheese. Season with salt, pepper, and grated nutmeg. Return the dish to the oven and finish baking until the top is crisp.

If you like, add shelled shrimp to this dish.

Marinated Mackerel
Maquereaux marinés

SERVES 6
PREPARATION TIME: 20 MINUTES
COOKING TIME: 10 MINUTES
CHILLING TIME: 1 HOUR

12 small mackerel, gutted and cleaned

Salt and freshly ground pepper

1 lemon, peeled and thinly sliced, for garnish

COOKED MARINADE

1 medium-sized carrot

1 large onion

Dry white wine

Vinegar

1 sprig thyme

½ bay leaf

Thinly slice the carrot and onion. Cook the marinade for 20 minutes: use two-thirds dry white wine, one-third vinegar, the thinly sliced carrot and onion, the thyme, and half a bay leaf.

Preheat the oven to 350°F (180°C). Arrange the mackerel in an ovenproof ceramic dish. Season them with salt and freshly ground pepper. Cover the mackerel with the marinade and cook for 8 to 10 minutes. Leave to cool in the dish and chill for about 1 hour.

To serve, garnish each mackerel with a thin slice of lemon.

SERVES 4
PREPARATION TIME: 30 MINUTES
COOKING TIME: 15 MINUTES

1 ⅔ cups (400 ml) milk

4 eggs, separated

2 teaspoons milk

¾ cup (2 ½ oz./75 g) flour

2 oz. (60 g) Parmesan or Gruyère cheese, grated

2 tablespoons (30 g) butter, plus extra for greasing the molds

Salt and pepper

Nutmeg to taste

Parmesan Soufflés
Soufflés au Parmesan

Preheat the oven to 350°F (180°C). Butter four small soufflé molds or porcelain ramekins. Bring the milk to a boil and leave it to cool a little. Dilute the egg yolks with the 2 teaspoons of milk. Then pour the slightly cooled milk little by little over the flour, stirring all the time, until you have a perfectly smooth mixture with no lumps. Season with salt, and add a pinch of pepper and a little nutmeg. Bring this back to a boil, stirring constantly. As soon as it begins boiling, remove the pan from the heat and immediately stir in the cheese, butter, and yolks diluted with milk.

Whisk the 4 egg whites to firm peaks and carefully fold them into the milk mixture. Make sure you don't deflate the whisked whites.

Fill each soufflé mold or ramekin three-quarters full and bake for 10 minutes. The soufflés should be well risen with a lovely crust. Serve immediately.

SERVES 6
PREPARATION TIME: 20 MINUTES
COOKING TIME: 30 MINUTES

2 cups (500 ml) Béchamel or White Sauce (see p. 54)

8 oz. (250 g) cooked lean ham

2 tablespoons (30 g) butter

1 pinch paprika

3 eggs, separated

Ham Soufflés
Soufflés au jambon

Preheat the oven to 350°F (180°C). Butter a soufflé dish or individual ramekins. Heat the béchamel sauce. Grind or process the ham finely with the butter. Push the mixture through a fine-meshed sieve and stir it into the hot béchamel sauce with the paprika. Incorporate the three egg yolks. Whisk the egg whites to firm peaks and fold them in carefully. Make sure you don't deflate the whisked whites. Fill the soufflé dish or ramekins three-quarters full and bake for about 30 minutes, until the batter has doubled in volume and risen well above the rim. Serve immediately.

SERVES 4
PREPARATION TIME: 10 MINUTES

1 medium head of curly-leaf
endive or escarole

2 cloves garlic

8 × 1 in. (2.5 cm) squares of
toasted bread (croutons)

1 teaspoon Dijon mustard

1 tablespoon red wine vinegar

2 tablespoons salad oil

Salt and pepper

Curly-Leaf Endive Salad
Frisée

Carefully wash, drain, and coarsely chop the endives.

Peel the cloves of garlic and slice them in half lengthwise. Rub each crouton with garlic. Set aside.

In a large salad bowl, whisk together the mustard, vinegar, oil, salt, and pepper. Then place the croutons in the bowl and stir to coat them with the dressing. Add the endives, toss, and serve immediately.

SERVES 4
PREPARATION TIME: 10 MINUTES
CHILLING TIME: 30 MINUTES

3 cucumbers weighing
1 ¼-1 ½ lb. (600 to 700 g)
in total

1 bunch chives

2 tablespoons crème fraîche
or heavy cream, or half an
individual plain yogurt

1 tablespoon lemon juice

Salt and pepper

Cucumber and Cream Salad
Concombres à la crème

Cucumbers are easier to digest if they have been peeled and salted before being used in salads.

Peel the cucumbers and cut them into slices. Place them on a large plate, salt, then turn the pieces over and salt again. Leave the cucumbers in the refrigerator for 30 minutes before making the salad.

Remove the cucumbers from the refrigerator, place in a colander, and rinse off under cold running water. Leave them to dry on a paper towel. Finely chop the chives. Make a sauce by stirring together the cream, lemon juice, chives, salt, and pepper. Place the cucumbers on individual plates, spoon the sauce over them, and serve.

Quiche Lorraine

SERVES 4
PREPARATION TIME: 20 MINUTES
RESTING TIME:
1 HOUR 30 MINUTES
COOKING TIME: 35 MINUTES

DOUGH

5 tablespoons (75 g) butter

1 ½ cups (150 g) flour

½ teaspoon (4 g) salt

2 tablespoons water

(A frozen crust can be used
instead.)

FILLING

4 oz. (125 g) slab bacon or
prosciutto

2 eggs

6 tablespoons (100 ml) crème
fraîche or heavy cream

1 oz. (30g) butter

Salt and pepper

Nutmeg

If you are preparing a crust from scratch, place the flour and salt in a large mixing bowl. Take the butter out of the refrigerator an hour before beginning the crust. Break the butter into the bowl in little nut-sized pieces, then use your fingers to "pinch" the flour and butter together. Work quickly to make a crumbly mixture, then add the water and quickly form the dough into a ball, working it as little as possible. Cover the ball of dough with a clean cloth and leave for 1 ½ hours before baking.

If you are using a frozen crust, simply defrost it.

Meanwhile, remove the rind from the bacon and cut into ½-in. (1-cm) cubes; or, if using prosciutto, cut into strips. Fry the bacon or prosciutto in an ungreased frying pan until the pieces have browned.

Preheat the oven to 450°F–475°F (240°C).

Roll out the dough on a well-floured surface to make a circle about ¼ in. (5 mm) thick. Lightly butter an 8-in. (20-cm) pie pan, line with the dough, and prick the bottom with a fork. Place the pieces of bacon evenly over the bottom, gently pushing them into the dough, then place in the oven for 15 minutes.

Whisk the eggs and cream together in a mixing bowl. Add a little salt, pepper, and nutmeg. When the 15 minutes of baking time is up, pour this mixture into the pie pan, dot with butter, lower the oven temperature to 300°F (150°C), and bake for 20 minutes more. If the quiche colors too much while baking, cover with a piece of aluminum foil.

Serve hot from the oven.

SERVES 5 TO 6
PREPARATION TIME: 30 MINUTES
COOKING TIME:
1 HOUR 20 MINUTES

1 dried pork sausage for cooking, weighing about 2 ¼ lb. (1 kg) and about 12 in. (30 cm) long (at specialty charcuterie counters)

1 cup (250 ml) Beaujolais wine or other fruity red wine

1 lb. (500 g) brioche dough

1 egg yolk

Flour for dusting

Brioche Sausage Roll
Saucisson en brioche

Place the dried sausage in cold water in a pan over minimum heat. Cook it, ensuring that the water does not boil, for 30 minutes. Then remove the pan from the heat and leave the sausage to cool a little. Preheat the oven to 475°F (240°C), or as high as your oven will go. While the sausage is still warm, remove it from the pan and peel off the casing. Roast it for a few minutes. The sausage will render some of its fat, which you should discard. Deglaze the dish with Beaujolais wine, return to the stovetop, and reduce until dry.

Roll out the brioche dough until it is just a little longer than the sausage, and is 6 in. (15 cm) wide. At this stage, you may reserve a little dough for decoration if you wish.

Brush the sausage with a little egg yolk and sprinkle it with flour. Brush the edge of the dough lightly with water to ensure that the two sides stick together, so that the brioche will stay firmly closed; then roll the sausage up in it. Brush the dough all over with the remaining egg yolk, and decorate it with a few cutout shapes of dough or simply with the tip of a knife.

Place the enclosed sausage on a baking tray and leave the dough to rise a little. Bake in a hot oven at 425°F (220°C) for about 30 minutes, until the brioche is a lovely golden color. To serve, cut into slices. A fine Périgueux sauce is an excellent accompaniment to this dish.

Note: Périgueux sauce is Madeira sauce to which finely chopped or diced truffles are added. It is named after the town of Périgueux in the Périgord region of France, renowned for its truffles.

3 ½ oz. (100 g) Gruyère cheese

4 tablespoons (60 g) butter, plus butter for the soufflé dish

Generous ½ cup (150 ml) water

1 scant cup (125 g) flour

3 eggs, separated

Salt

Nutmeg

Gougère

Preheat the oven to 425°F (210°C).

Grate the Gruyère cheese and set aside.

Melt the butter with a little salt in a saucepan, then pour in the water and bring to a boil. Add the flour all at once, stirring constantly until the batter is smooth, detaches from the sides of the saucepan, and forms a ball around the spoon. Remove the pan from the heat and beat in the egg yolks one by one; then stir in the grated cheese and a little nutmeg.

Lightly butter a 6-in. (15-cm) soufflé mold or four individual ramekins, and place in the oven while finishing the batter.

Beat the egg whites until stiff, add a quarter of them to the batter, stirring them in with the whisk; then incorporate the rest of the egg whites in the same way. Remember to keep an eye on the buttered mold(s)—the butter should just start to brown lightly. Remove the mold(s) from the oven, pour in the batter, return to the oven, and bake for 25 minutes or until the blade of the knife comes out clean when stuck into the center of the gougère. Serve as soon as it comes out of the oven.

Serving suggestions: A gougère can be served alone as an entrée or as an accompaniment to meat, especially roast beef or lamb.

Chicken Salad
Poulet en salade

SERVES 4
PREPARATION TIME: 25 MINUTES

Both breasts from a roasted or
boiled chicken

1 small butterhead (Boston)
lettuce

Tender pale leaves from
a curly-leaf endive

1 celery heart (tender part
of innermost ribs)

3 ½ oz. (100 g) Gruyère cheese

4 new baby onions

1 clove garlic (optional)

3 large tomatoes

1 scant cup (100 g) black olives

1 cup (100 g) walnut meats

1 tablespoon sherry vinegar

3 tablespoons olive oil

Salt and pepper

Carefully wash, and coarsely chop the lettuce and endive leaves. Wash and dice the celery into cubes of roughly ½ in. (1 cm). Dice the Gruyère cheese. Peel and finely slice the onions. Peel and finely chop the garlic (if using).

Cut the chicken breasts into strips.

Run the tomatoes under hot water, peel them, and chop them.

Place the chicken, lettuce, endives, celery, onion, cheese, olives, tomatoes, and nuts all in a salad bowl and chill until ready to serve.

In a small bowl, whisk together the vinegar, oil, salt, pepper, and garlic (if using). Pour over the salad, toss, and serve immediately.

Note: This salad could be a meal in itself–it's especially nice on a summer evening.

SERVES 4
PREPARATION TIME:
1 HOUR 15 MINUTES

Cantaloupe and Prosciutto
Melons et jambon de Parme

4 small or 2 large cantaloupes
Crushed ice
8 very thin slices prosciutto

Make sure your melons are perfectly ripe. If you keep them in the refrigerator, it is best to first place them in a plastic bag because a truly ripe melon will impregnate everything with its aroma. Otherwise, place the uncut melons in a large bowl of ice water and leave for 1 hour before serving.

This dish can be served in various ways; I find the following one particularly attractive. Place some crushed ice on a large serving platter. If using small canteloupes, cut off the very top of each one just below the stem and reserve. Scoop out all the seeds with a spoon, then place two slices of ham around the opening of each melon, pleating it so it will look like a fancy collar coming out of the melon. Place the "top" with the stem back in place and serve.

If the melons are large, simply cut them in half, scoop out the seeds, place the ham in each half as described above, and serve.

Serving suggestions: This is delicious served with a glass of red port.

Sauces & Condiments

Foamy Butter Sauce
Beurre blanc

SERVES 4 TO 6
PREPARATION TIME: 10 MINUTES
COOKING TIME: 10 MINUTES

1 ¾ sticks (200 g) softened butter
2 shallots
2 tablespoons red wine vinegar
Salt and pepper

At least three hours ahead of time, take the butter out of the refrigerator to soften at room temperature.

Peel the shallots and finely chop them on a cutting board.

A thick-bottomed saucepan that holds the heat is preferable for making this sauce.

Place the shallots and vinegar in a small heavy-bottomed saucepan and boil until the vinegar has evaporated and the shallots are simply moist in the bottom of the pan. Break the butter into pieces. Lift the saucepan off of the heat and begin rapidly stirring in the butter a piece at a time using a wooden spoon. The sauce should become creamy as the butter is added; it should not become overheated or the butter will boil. Place the pot on the top of a double boiler to keep the sauce warm; stir constantly, removing the pot from the heat as the butter is being added. Once all the butter has been added, beat the sauce with a whisk to make it foamy.

Season to taste with salt and pepper and serve.

Serving suggestions: Serve with poached fish, especially salmon and pike.

Béarnaise Sauce
Sauce béarnaise

SERVES 4 TO 6
PREPARATION TIME: 10 MINUTES
COOKING TIME: 15 MINUTES

3 medium shallots

3 tablespoons white wine vinegar

2 tablespoons chopped tarragon

1 pinch chopped chervil

4 egg yolks

2 ¼ sticks (250 g) unsalted butter

Salt and freshly crushed pepper

This sauce must be made over very low heat, just before serving. Making it in a double boiler will ensure good results. Use the top of the double boiler as an ordinary pot for the first stage of making the sauce.

Peel and finely chop the shallots. Place the vinegar, shallots, chopped tarragon and chervil (setting aside a little of both for the end), a little salt, and a pinch of freshly crushed pepper in the top part of the double boiler. Place over high heat and reduce until you have the equivalent of 2 teaspoons left in the pan. Remove from the heat and leave to cool completely before finishing the sauce (you can speed cooling by holding the pot in a bowl of ice water).

Whisk the egg yolks, one by one, and 2 tablespoons of cold water into the vinegar mixture. Heat a little water in the bottom of the double boiler and set the top part in place.

Break the butter into small pieces. Whisk in a piece of the butter, then continue adding the rest of the butter little by little, whisking constantly. The sauce should become foamy at first, then thicken as the butter is added. Keep warm over a warm hot-water bath.

Just before serving, add salt and pepper, if needed, and the remaining tarragon and chervil. Serve in a sauceboat.

Note: This sauce should be much thicker than a Hollandaise sauce; it has more egg yolks. It should have the consistency of Dijon mustard.

Serving suggestions: This is the perfect sauce for any grilled meat.

2 ¼ lb. (1 kg) unsalted
butter, softened

2 oz. (50 g) garlic

1 ½ oz. (40 g) shallots

⅔ oz. (20 g) kosher salt

1 generous pinch (1 g) freshly
ground pepper

1 pinch freshly ground nutmeg

1 ¾ oz. (50 g) almonds

3 ½ oz. (100 g) parsley

Snail Butter
Beurre d'escargots

Peel the garlic cloves and crush them with the back of a knife.
Finely chop the shallots. Combine the salt, pepper, nutmeg,
garlic, shallots, and almonds in a food processor and combine
until they form a smooth paste. Alternatively, use a mortar and
pestle. Chop the parsley finely and incorporate it, with the softened butter, into the paste.

Keep chilled until needed.

Gribiche Sauce
Sauce gribiche

SERVES 5 TO 6
PREPARATION TIME: 25 MINUTES
COOKING TIME: 11 TO 12 MINUTES

5 eggs

2 tablespoons vinegar

1 ⅔ cups (400 ml) oil

1 teaspoon chopped chervil

1 teaspoon chopped tarragon

1 teaspoon capers

1 teaspoon Dijon mustard

3 medium-sized gherkins

Salt and pepper

Place the 5 eggs in a saucepan of gently simmering water. Leave to simmer until hard-boiled, about 11 to 12 minutes, then remove and cool immediately under cold running water.

Cut the eggs open and scoop out the yolks. Reserve the whites. Place the yolks in a bowl with salt and pepper and crush finely. Drizzle in the vinegar and then the oil, very slowly, just as you would to make mayonnaise. To ensure that the texture is creamy, add a little vinegar or warm water if necessary. Finely dice the egg whites. Lastly, add the chopped herbs, capers, mustard, chopped gherkins, and egg whites. Adjust the seasoning.

Note: This sauce is really a mayonnaise in which the egg yolks are cooked instead of raw.

SERVES 4
PREPARATION TIME: 10 MINUTES
COOKING TIME: 45 MINUTES

1 lb. (500 g) ripe tomatoes

1 small bouquet garni, made with 1 bunch parsley, 1 sprig tarragon, 2 sprigs thyme, and ¼ bay leaf

1 medium onion

1 clove garlic

6 tablespoons (100 ml) olive oil

1 teaspoon (5 g) granulated sugar

Salt and pepper

Tomato Sauce
Sauce tomate

The better the tomatoes, the better the sauce, so use perfectly ripe ones. Wash them, cut each one in half, and squeeze gently to remove the seeds.

Wash the parsley and the tarragon, and tie them together with the bay leaf and thyme to form the bouquet garni. Peel the onion and the garlic, and slice the onion.

Heat the olive oil in a large saucepan; add the garlic, onion, tomatoes, and bouquet garni. Cook uncovered over moderate heat at a rapid boil, crushing the tomatoes at first, then stirring occasionally with a wooden spoon for 35 minutes, or until the water in the tomatoes has evaporated and a thick sauce is formed.

Stir in the sugar, then grind the sauce through a food mill or purée in a blender or food processor. Taste for salt and pepper. If the sauce seems too thin at this point, you can boil it some more to thicken; otherwise it is ready to serve.

This sauce keeps well–up to a week refrigerated in a glass jar or bottle if you add a tablespoon of olive oil on top before closing the container.

Serving suggestions: Serve with pasta, white beans, fish dumplings, or ravioli.

Aïoli Sauce
Sauce aïoli

SERVES 4
PREPARATION TIME: 10 MINUTES

8 cloves garlic

2 egg yolks

1 ¼ cups (300 ml) oil

Juice of ½ lemon

Salt

Crush the garlic using a mortar and pestle until they form a paste. Incorporate the egg yolks into the garlic paste and add a pinch of salt. Slowly drizzle the oil in, turning the pestle as you do so. To maintain the creamy consistency, add a few drops of lemon juice (the acidic element) from time to time and a few drops of warm water.

Béchamel or White Sauce
Sauce blanche

PREPARATION TIME: 15 MINUTES
COOKING TIME: UP TO
15 MINUTES

3 tablespoons (50 g) butter

2 tablespoons (20 g) flour

1 cup (250 ml) cold milk

Generous ¾ cup (200 ml) crème fraîche or heavy cream

Nutmeg, salt, and pepper

1 teaspoon lemon juice (optional)

Melt the butter in a medium-size saucepan (enameled cast iron is excellent). Add the flour and stir until smooth over low heat; the flour should not brown. Pour in all of the cold milk at once, then bring to a boil, stirring constantly.

Lower the heat and cook at a gentle boil for 8 minutes, stirring occasionally, then add the cream, a little nutmeg, salt, pepper, and the lemon juice (if desired). Stir and cook for a minute or two more; the sauce should coat the spoon when done.

Serve immediately, or keep warm in a double boiler for later use.

Serving suggestions: Use this sauce to make gratinéed vegetables; just pour the sauce over cooked vegetables and place in a very hot oven for 15 to 20 minutes to brown.

SERVES 4
PREPARATION TIME: 10 MINUTES
COOKING TIME: 5 MINUTES

3 tablespoons (50 g) softened butter

2 tablespoons lemon juice

2 egg yolks

1 tablespoon cold water

1 generous tablespoon Dijon mustard

Salt and pepper

1 tablespoon chopped parsley (optional) or 1 tablespoon capers (optional)

Mustard Sauce
Sauce moutarde

It's best to use a double boiler to make this sauce.

Heat a little water in the bottom of the double boiler. Break the butter into ten pieces. Place the butter, lemon juice, egg yolks, and a little salt and pepper in the top; set over the hot water and whisk vigorously until the mixture begins to thicken. Whisk in the cold water, remove the sauce from the heat, pour into a clean bowl, and allow to cool completely.

Once the sauce is cold, stir in the mustard and serve.

Serving suggestions: A tablespoon of chopped parsley may be added to the sauce just before serving with grilled meats, or a tablespoon of capers to go with grilled fish.

SERVES 4
PREPARATION TIME: 5 MINUTES

1 teaspoon Dijon mustard

1 tablespoon red wine vinegar

2 tablespoons salad oil

Salt and pepper

Vinaigrette

Place the mustard and vinegar in a mixing bowl and stir to combine, then add the oil in a steady stream, stirring as it is being added. Season with salt and pepper–the sauce is ready to use.

Variations: Vary your vinaigrettes by using different oils and different acids. For instance, use olive oil or walnut oil, sherry vinegar or lemon juice, or a mixture of vinegar and lemon juice.

Serving suggestions: Use with any salad greens, or with cold boiled vegetables, such as asparagus.

SERVES 4
PREPARATION TIME: 15 MINUTES
COOKING TIME: 15 MINUTES

1 ¼ sticks (150 g) softened butter

1 ½ teaspoons wine vinegar
(preferably white wine vinegar)

2 egg yolks

2 tablespoons lemon juice

Salt and pepper

Hollandaise Sauce
Hollandaise vite faite

Take the butter out of the refrigerator an hour ahead of time to soften. Break the butter into ten pieces.

As for Béarnaise Sauce (see p. 47), for the best results, it is advisable to make this sauce in a double boiler.

Heat a little water in the bottom of a double boiler. Place the vinegar and egg yolks in the top, whisk to combine, and season lightly with salt and pepper. Continue whisking and add the butter, a piece at a time. Once all the butter has been added, whisk in the lemon juice (more may be added to taste, if desired). Heat for 5 minutes longer, stirring constantly. Taste for salt and pepper and serve.

It is best to serve this sauce immediately, but it may be kept warm in the double boiler, away from the heat, if need be.

A variation on this sauce, called mousseline sauce, can be made by whipping 3 tablespoons of heavy cream until stiff and stirring it into the warm sauce just before serving.

In any case, do not allow to overheat and certainly do not boil.

Serving suggestions: Hollandaise is excellent with any poached fish or with boiled vegetables, such as asparagus or broccoli.

Sweet and Sour Pickled Cherries
Cerises à l'aigre-doux

FOR THREE 1-QUART (1-LITER) JARS
PREPARATION TIME: 20 MINUTES
COOKING TIME: 15 MINUTES
MARINATING TIME: 2 WEEKS

4 ½ lb. (2 kg) fresh cherries

4 sprigs fresh tarragon (see Note)

3 tablespoons (40 g) granulated sugar

20 peppercorns

1 ¼ quarts (1 ¼ liter) crystal (white) vinegar, 8 percent strength

Wash the cherries and dry them on a clean towel. Cut each cherry stem in half. Carefully wash and dry the sprigs of tarragon.

Carefully wash and dry the jars, then place the cherries in them as tightly as possible without crushing them. Put a tablespoon of sugar, a sprig of tarragon, and 5 peppercorns in each jar as well.

Boil the vinegar gently for 15 minutes with another branch of tarragon and 5 peppercorns. Then strain it and pour enough into each jar of fruit that the fruit is completely immersed. Leave the jars in a dark place (such as a kitchen cabinet) until the vinegar has cooled completely. Then seal the jars with a lid or a piece of waxed paper and a rubber band.

The cherries are ready to eat in 2 weeks.

Serving suggestions: Serve with cold meats, salads, or appetizers.

Note: If fresh tarragon is unavailable, ½ teaspoon dried tarragon may be added to each jar and to the vinegar instead.

Eggs

SERVES 4
PREPARATION TIME: 10 MINUTES
COOKING TIME: 15 MINUTES

7 eggs

3 ½ oz. (100 g) slab bacon

2 medium (10 oz./300 g) potatoes, boiled

3 tablespoons (40 g) butter

Salt and pepper

1 tablespoon cold water

Potato and Bacon Omelet
Omelette aux pommes de terre et au lard

About one hour ahead of time, take the eggs out of the refrigerator.

Remove the bacon rind and dice the bacon. Fry the bacon in a very large ungreased frying pan. Cook slowly so that the fat will melt and the bacon will brown; turn the pieces over several times for even browning.

Dice or thinly slice the potatoes.

Remove the bacon from the pan and place on a paper towel to drain. Discard the fat. Wipe the frying pan with a clean paper towel, then melt the butter in it. When the butter starts to foam, add the potatoes and brown over moderate heat, turning them over carefully so they do not break. Break the eggs into a mixing bowl, season with salt and pepper, add 1 tablespoon of cold water, and beat with a fork just enough to break the yolks and mix them slightly with the whites; they should not be well mixed. Put the pieces of bacon back into the pan, then add the eggs. Cook for 5 to 6 minutes, or until done. Then slide the omelet onto a warm serving platter, giving it a gentle flip so that it will fold over onto itself. Serve immediately, accompanied by a green salad.

Variation: The omelet may be cooked separately and the browned bacon and potatoes added afterward, once the omelet has been slid onto the serving platter.

Note: The omelet is done when the surface is set and creamy but not dry.

Creamy Scrambled Eggs with Salmon
Oeufs brouillés au saumon fumé

SERVES 4
PREPARATION TIME: 5 MINUTES
COOKING TIME: 8 TO 10 MINUTES

2 thin slices (4 oz./115 g) smoked salmon

2 tablespoons (30 g) butter

8 eggs

6 tablespoons (100 ml) crème fraîche or heavy cream

Salt and pepper

8 slices toasted country-style or whole-wheat bread

At least one hour ahead of time, take all the ingredients out of the refrigerator.

Cut the salmon into thin strips.

Melt the butter in a double boiler. Whisk the eggs just enough to mix, and add the salmon, salt, and pepper. Pour the eggs into the butter and stir with a wooden spoon until very thick and creamy. Add the cream, stir to combine, and remove from the heat. Season with a little more pepper. Serve with buttered toast.

Note: Eggs scrambled in this way are not stiff but thick and creamy (almost like a sauce), so you may prefer to serve them in bowls and eat them with a spoon.

SERVES 4
PREPARATION TIME: 10 MINUTES
COOKING TIME: 15 TO
20 MINUTES

10 eggs

5 oz. (150 g) truffles

2 tablespoons (30 g) butter, plus
a little extra to make the toast

8 round pieces bread

Salt and pepper

Scrambled Eggs with Truffles
Oeufs brouillés aux truffes

Butter 4 small dariole molds and place one generous slice of truffle in each. Dice the remaining truffles and stew them in butter.

Prepare creamy scrambled eggs with 6 of the eggs. Incorporate the diced truffles. Add the 4 remaining raw eggs. As you mix them in, season with salt and pepper.

Fill the molds with the mixture and poach them in a bain-marie for 15 to 20 minutes. While they are cooking, brown the slices of bread in clarified butter.

Serve accompanied by a very light *demi-glace* sauce flavored with truffle essence.

This dish is known as oeufs moulés Verdi, *Verdi molded eggs.*

Eggs *en Cocotte* with Tomatoes
Oeufs en cocotte aux tomates

SERVES 4
PREPARATION TIME: 10 MINUTES
COOKING TIME: 20 MINUTES

1 onion (optional), plus butter for cooking

2 ripe tomatoes

1 tablespoon plus 1 teaspoon (20 g) butter, divided

4 eggs

A few leaves of flat-leaf parsley, chopped

Salt and pepper

If using, chop the onion finely and soften it in butter without browning it. Set aside. Remove the base from the tomatoes and dip them very briefly in boiling water. Peel them immediately, cut them in two, and remove the seeds.

Dice the tomatoes and sauté them in the same pan with half the butter (2 teaspoons or 10 g). Season with salt and pepper. Cook until the tomatoes are reduced to the texture of preserves.

Preheat the oven to 375°F (190°C).

Butter the ramekins and smooth the puréed tomatoes into the bottom, setting aside a little for garnish. Break an egg into each dish and place in a dish of hot water. Bake for about 20 minutes, until the whites are coagulated. As soon as they are done, drop in a half-teaspoon of puréed tomatoes and sprinkle with a little chopped parsley.

If you are using onion, add it to the ramekin before spooning in the tomato purée.

SERVES 4
PREPARATION TIME: 20 MINUTES
COOKING TIME: 20 MINUTES

Soft-Boiled Eggs Béarnaise
Oeufs mollets béarnaise

2 tablespoons (30 g) butter

8 artichoke bottoms

8 soft-boiled eggs

1 ⅔ cups (400 ml) Béarnaise Sauce (see p. 47)

Salt and freshly ground pepper

If you are using fresh artichokes, simmer the bottoms in water with lemon juice and a little flour (a *blanc*) until slightly softened but not cooked through.

Melt the butter in a sauté pan and add the artichoke bottoms. Season with a pinch of salt and freshly ground pepper and leave to simmer for 15 minutes over low heat, turning them once. Transfer them to a pre-heated dish and pour in the butter from the pan.

Place a shelled soft-boiled egg in each artichoke bottom and cover with the béarnaise sauce, serving the remaining sauce in a dish on the side.

Bacon and Eggs
Oeufs au bacon

SERVES 4
PREPARATION TIME:
5 TO 10 MINUTES
COOKING TIME: 15 MINUTES

8 thin slices Canadian bacon or
4 slices ham cut in half

4 tablespoons (60 g) butter

8 eggs

Salt and pepper

8 slices toast

Ideally, use individual porcelain or enameled cast-iron dishes to cook this dish.

At least one hour ahead of time, take all the ingredients out of the refrigerator.

Brown the Canadian bacon or ham in a nonstick frying pan for about 5 minutes.

Melt 1 tablespoon (15 g) of butter in each of the individual dishes, then place two pieces of bacon or ham in each one.

Break the eggs into a small bowl, two at a time, then carefully slide them into each dish. Salt and pepper lightly. Cook over very low heat for about 4 minutes, or until the white is half cooked; then raise the heat and finish cooking for about 3 minutes.

Serve with toast, either as an appetizer or for breakfast, accompanied by tea or coffee and fresh fruit juice.

SERVES 4
PREPARATION TIME: 15 MINUTES
COOKING TIME: 15 MINUTES

8 eggs

About 5 oz. (150 g) chanterelle mushrooms (see Note)

5 tablespoons (75 g) butter, divided

6 tablespoons (100 ml) crème fraîche or heavy cream

Salt and pepper

8 slices toast

Creamy Scrambled Eggs with Chanterelles
Oeufs brouillés aux chanterelles

At least one hour ahead of time, take the eggs out of the refrigerator.

Cut off any dirt from the base of each mushroom, then wash them quickly, drain, and dry on a towel.

Melt 2 tablespoons (30 g) of butter in a frying pan over moderate heat, and add the mushrooms. At first, they will release some liquid; as soon as this liquid has evaporated, lower the heat and simmer (the butter absorbed by the mushrooms will now reappear in the pan).

Melt 3 tablespoons (45 g) of butter in the top of a double boiler. Break the eggs into a bowl, add salt and pepper, whisk lightly, then pour into the melted butter. Continue whisking until the eggs are creamy; then stir in the cream with a wooden spoon. Stir constantly as the eggs are cooking, so they won't stick to the pan; when they are thick and creamy and coat the spoon, they are done.

Remove the double boiler from the heat and stir the mushrooms into the eggs. Serve immediately with buttered toast.

Note: Although chanterelles are called for here, many other wild mushrooms could be used instead (e.g., boletus, Japanese shitake mushrooms). About ½ cup (15 g) top-quality dried wild mushrooms may also be used. Soak them for about 20 minutes in warm water (or follow the directions on the package), then add them with 6 tablespoons (100 ml) of their water to the melted butter and cook as described for the fresh mushrooms.

Wild Mushroom Omelet
Omelette aux champignons

SERVES 4
PREPARATION TIME: 10 MINUTES
COOKING TIME: 35 MINUTES

8 eggs

8 oz. (250 g) fresh wild mushrooms, preferably morels (see Note)

3 tablespoons (40 g) butter

Salt and pepper

At least one hour ahead of time, take all the ingredients out of the refrigerator.

Cut off any dirt from the stems of the mushrooms, then wash the mushrooms and cut them in half lengthwise or into slices. Melt half the butter in a very large frying pan. Add the mushrooms, salt, and pepper, and cook over moderate heat, stirring frequently, until all the liquid from the mushrooms has evaporated (about 10 to 15 minutes).

Break the eggs into a mixing bowl, season with salt and pepper, and beat lightly with a fork. Pour the mushrooms into the bowl with the eggs.

Melt the remaining butter in the pan. When hot, pour in the egg and mushroom mixture and cook for 5 to 10 minutes, or until done. Slide the omelet out of the pan and onto a warm serving platter, giving the pan a gentle flip when the omelet is halfway onto the platter so that it will fold over onto itself. Serve immediately.

Note: Although morels are called for in this recipe, many other wild mushrooms could be used instead (e.g., boletus, Japanese shitake mushrooms). About ¾ cup (25 g) top-quality dried wild mushrooms may also be used. Soak them for about 20 minutes in warm water (or follow the directions on the package), then add them with ½ cup (120 ml) of their water to the melted butter and cook as described for the fresh mushrooms.

Unless you have a very large frying pan, make two omelets, using half the egg and mushroom mixture each time.

Fish

SERVES 4
PREPARATION TIME: 20 MINUTES
COOKING TIME: 40 MINUTES

1 large piece cod, about 1 ½ lb. (600 g), preferably cut from the central, thick part of the body

14 oz. (400 g) new potatoes

3 ½ oz. (100 g) small new onions

3 tablespoons (50 g) butter, melted

1 tablespoon olive oil (optional)

1 pinch chopped parsley

1 lemon, quartered

Salt and pepper

Baked Cod
Cabillaud à la ménagère

Preheat the oven to 350°F (180°C).

Scale and wash the fish.

Generously butter an earthenware dish large enough to hold the fish and the vegetables. Season the fish all over generously with salt and pepper. Arrange small new potatoes and onions around it. If the vegetables are not new, first boil them briefly, drain, and season with table salt. Drizzle the melted butter over the fish and vegetables and cook in the oven, spooning frequently with the cooking liquid–if you like you can add 1 tablespoon of olive oil to it. The onions should comprise one quarter of the total garnish. Make sure that they stand firmly on the base of the dish so that they are in constant contact with the buttery cooking juices. This way, they will turn a nice golden color.

Just before serving the fish in the cooking dish, sprinkle the fish and vegetables with the freshly chopped parsley. On the side, serve the lemon quarters to squeeze over the fish when it is served into warmed plates.

Poaching and grilling are two other cooking methods that are very suitable for cod. Cut it into 1-in. (2-cm) slices and serve it with one of the sauces recommended for poached or grilled fish.

SERVES 6 TO 8
PREPARATION TIME: 1 HOUR
COOKING TIME:
1 HOUR 30 MINUTES

1 Mediterranean sea bass, weighing about 6 ½ lb. (3 kg)

5 sprigs chervil, leaves picked

5 sprigs tarragon, leaves picked

2 pieces puff pastry large enough to encase the fish

1 egg yolk, lightly beaten

Salt and pepper

Mediterranean Sea Bass in a Pastry Case
Loup de la Méditerranée en croûte

Gut the fish and remove the skin, being careful not to damage the flesh and leaving the head and tail intact. Make an incision along the back until you reach the central bone. Insert leaves of freshly picked chervil and tarragon into the opening. Season with salt and pepper and close up the fish. Repeat the procedure at the stomach.

Preheat the oven to 425°F (220°C).

Roll out the two pieces of puff pastry until they are a little longer and wider than the fish. Place the fish on one of them and cover it with the other. To seal the fish within the pastry case, simply press the two sides of pastry together all around the fish so that its shape can be clearly seen.

Using a very thin knife, cut away the surplus pastry and use a little of it to shape the fin. Draw a few lines lengthways on the fin and use the remaining pastry to shape the gills and an eye. Baste the pastry with the egg yolk, then draw out the scales, using a very small, half-moon-shaped cooking cutter. This is fine work that requires a great deal of patience and skill.

Place the sea bass on a baking dish in the hot oven. As soon as the pastry begins to color, lower the temperature to 350°F (180°C) so that the encased fish can cook evenly and to avoid burning the pastry. Cook for about 1 hour 30 minutes.

To serve, place on a serving platter and cut it at the table. Accompany with melted butter or Foamy Butter Sauce (see p. 46).

Variation: Before wrapping in pastry, you may also stuff the sea bass with a delicate lobster mousse.

Roasted Monkfish
Rôti de lotte

SERVES 4
PREPARATION TIME: 10 MINUTES
COOKING TIME: 20 MINUTES

A 1 ¾ lb. (800 g) piece (preferably toward the tail) of monkfish (anglerfish), skinned

1 large clove garlic

¼ cup (60 ml) olive oil

1 tablespoon lemon juice

Salt and pepper

Preheat the oven to 450°F-475°F (240°C), or as high as your oven will go. Pat the fish dry with a clean towel. Peel the garlic and cut it into quarters. Lard the fish with garlic by making four incisions with a knife and sliding a piece of garlic into each one. Place the fish in a roasting pan, pour the oil over it, then roll the fish in the oil. Add the lemon juice, and sprinkle with salt and pepper.

Bake in the oven for 20 minutes, basting from time to time. Serve the fish in the dish in which it was cooked.

Turbot with Mixed Vegetables
Turbotin aux légumes

SERVES 4
PREPARATION TIME: 15 MINUTES
COOKING TIME: 10 MINUTES

1 turbot (or other flatfish) weighing 3 ½ lb. (1.5 kg)

2 carrots

¼ celeriac

1 leek

4 tablespoons (60 g) softened butter

Bouquet garni, made with 2 sprigs thyme, ¼ bay leaf, and 2 sprigs parsley tied together

1 cup (250 ml) dry white wine

Salt and pepper

Ask the fish seller to cut off the head and fins, and to cut the fish into four pieces.

Preheat the oven to 425°F (210°C). Bring water and salt to boil in a pot. Peel and wash the vegetables, and on a cutting board slice them into fine julienne strips.

Cook all the vegetables in the pot of lightly salted boiling water for 7 to 8 minutes, drain, cool under running water, and pat dry with a clean cloth. Butter a baking dish, spread the vegetables over the bottom, and place the pieces of fish on top. Season with salt and pepper, and place the bouquet garni in the dish. Add the white wine and bake in the oven for about 10 minutes. To serve, remove the bouquet garni and serve the fish and vegetables in the baking dish.

Serving suggestions: Serve with rice or fresh pasta.

Fresh Tuna and Tomatoes
Rôti de thon

SERVES 4
PREPARATION TIME: 15 MINUTES
COOKING TIME: 30 MINUTES

1 ¾ lb. (800 g) fresh tuna, in one piece (see Note)

2 medium (200 g) onions

3 medium (400 g) ripe tomatoes

¼ cup (60 ml) olive oil

1 clove garlic, whole and unpeeled

Bouquet garni, made of thyme, bay leaf, and parsley

Generous ½ cup (150 ml) dry white wine

Salt and pepper

Chopped tarragon (optional)

Peel and slice the onions. Peel the tomatoes and cut them into quarters.

Heat the oil in a large frying pan, brown the tuna on both sides, add the onion, and allow to color lightly, then add the tomatoes, garlic, and bouquet garni.

Cook over moderate heat for 15 minutes, turning once; then add the wine, salt, and pepper. Cover the pan and finish cooking over low heat for 15 minutes more.

Just before serving, sprinkle with the fresh tarragon (if desired).

Serving suggestions: Serve with rice or steamed potatoes.

Note: Red tuna is best. Try to get a slice from the middle of the fish if possible.

Any large, meaty fish, such as swordfish, can be cooked in the same way.

Cod Lyonnaise
Morue à la lyonnaise

SERVES 4
SOAKING TIME: 24 TO 48 HOURS
PREPARATION TIME: 20 MINUTES
COOKING TIME: 40 MINUTES

1 lb. (500 g) salted cod

3 medium-sized potatoes

3 medium-sized onions

1 tablespoon plus 1 teaspoon (20 g) butter

2 tablespoons oil

1 pinch fresh chopped parsley

½ tablespoon vinegar

Salt and pepper

Salt cod should be purchased in large, flattened, and dried pieces on the bone with the skin still attached. If unavailable, fillets may be used. In either case, before cooking, the fish should be cut into large pieces and soaked for 24 hours using the following method: turn a plate upside down in a large bowl or pot so that the fish does not rest directly on the bottom (all the salt falls to the bottom), and place the fish, skin side up, on top of it. Fill the bowl or pot with cold water and add a few ice cubes; change the water at least four times (six to eight is preferable) and add a few ice cubes each time. Before cooking, drain the cod and pat it dry with a clean cloth.

Poach the salted cod and remove the skin and bones. Flake it and dry it at low heat until all the cooking water has evaporated.

Peel the potatoes and cook them in salted water. Cut them into slices.

Finely cut the onions into julienne slices and sauté with the butter and oil. When they are cooked and only barely colored, add the cooked potatoes and sauté them until lightly browned.

Then add the prepared cod and sauté for a few moments over high heat. Check the seasoning and add some freshly ground pepper.

Just before serving, scatter the cod with the chopped parsley. Transfer to the serving platter and bring the vinegar to a boil rapidly in the sauté pan. Pour it over the cod.

SERVES 4
SOAKING TIME: 6 HOURS
PREPARATION TIME: 25 MINUTES
COOKING TIME: 25 MINUTES

1 ¾ lb. (800 g) smoked haddock

1 quart (1 liter) milk

½ medium onion, sliced

Bouquet garni made of thyme, bay leaf, and parsley

1 large tomato

1 clove garlic

2 onions

5½ tablespoons (80 g) butter

A pinch of saffron

1 tablespoon flour

Generous ½ cup (150 ml) dry white wine

6 tablespoons (100 ml) crème fraîche or heavy cream

Salt and pepper

Smoked Haddock with Cream Sauce
Haddock à la crème

Peel off the skin of the haddock (if there is any), and cut it into four or eight pieces. Place the fish on a platter or in a bowl. Add milk (enough to cover), the slices of onion, and the bouquet garni. Allow to soak for 6 hours (this will desalt the fish and make it tender).

Run the tomato under boiling water, peel it, finely chop it and set aside in a bowl. Peel and finely chop the garlic and onions on a cutting board.

Drain the haddock and pat it dry with a clean cloth. Melt the butter in a large frying pan. When it foams up, add the fish, and cook for 5 minutes on each side over moderate heat, shaking the pan constantly to keep it from sticking. Lift the cooked fish out of the pan with a slotted spatula, place it on a serving platter, cover, and keep warm while making the sauce.

Add the tomato, garlic, and onions to the pan, and simmer for 5 minutes. Sprinkle in the saffron and flour, stir to combine, then add the wine, stirring constantly. Simmer very gently for 8 minutes. Stir in the cream and continue cooking very slowly, over very low heat, for 5 to 6 minutes more. Add pepper, salt if needed, then strain the sauce, stirring and pressing on the vegetables to extract all the liquid. Pour the sauce over the fish and serve immediately. Serve with rice or steamed potatoes.

Note: Unless you have a very large frying pan, it will be necessary to cook the haddock in two batches. In this case, use half of the butter each time. If you prefer, the sauce may be spooned onto the plates and the fish placed on top to serve (see photograph).

SERVES 6
PREPARATION TIME: 15 MINUTES
COOKING TIME: 50 MINUTES

3 ½ lb. (1.5 kg) carp

3 shallots

1 small bunch parsley

4 medium (100 g) button
mushrooms

3 ½ tablespoons (50 g) softened
butter

1 ¼ cups (300 ml) dry white wine

Salt and pepper

Baked Carp
Carpe au four

Ask the fish seller to scale and clean the carp.

Preheat the oven to 350°F (180°C).

Peel the shallots. Wash the parsley and remove its stems. Chop the shallots and the parsley separately. Cut any dirt off the stems of the mushrooms, carefully wash them and then slice them.

Use the butter to grease a baking dish–either earthenware or porcelain–just large enough to hold the carp comfortably. Salt and pepper the fish inside and out, then place it in the dish. Around the fish, arrange the shallots, mushrooms, any roe or milt that was inside the fish, and half the parsley. Then sprinkle everything with salt and pepper. Add the wine and bake for 50 minutes, basting occasionally. Five minutes before the fish is done, sprinkle the remaining parsley over it.

Serve the fish in the cooking dish.

SERVES 6
PREPARATION TIME: 10 MINUTES
COOKING TIME: 15 MINUTES

Red Mullet en Papillote
Rougets en papillotes

6 red mullet (goatfish)
weighing about 9 oz.
(250 g) each

3 shallots

2 medium tomatoes

4 large button mushrooms

2 tablespoons olive oil

Fennel seeds

Salt and pepper

1 lemon

Preheat the oven to 350°F (180°C).

Scale the fish and remove the gills, but don't clean otherwise. Peel and finely chop the shallots. Blanch the tomatoes, peel them, and chop them. Wash the mushrooms in water with a little lemon juice squeezed in and slice them. Set all the vegetables aside. Brush the fish with oil, then place each one on a piece of aluminum foil or parchment paper about 14 in. (35 cm) square. Use a sharp knife to make several little incisions in the sides of each fish, and insert one or two fennel seeds into each cut. Place a little tomato, shallot, and mushroom over and under each fish and season with salt and pepper. Then fold and squeeze the edges of the foil or parchment together to enclose the fish. Don't wrap the fish too tightly: there should be a pocket of air above each one to allow the steam to circulate while the fish is cooking.

Once all the fish are wrapped up, place them on a baking sheet and bake in the oven for 15 minutes. Cut the lemon into quarters.

Serve the fish hot in the foil or parchment they baked in, with wedges of lemon on the side.

Serving suggestions: Serve with melted butter sauce or Mustard Sauce (see p. 56) in a sauceboat on the side.

Note: Other fish can be cooked in exactly the same way but they should be cleaned before cooking.

Raw Salmon Renga-Ya
Saumon cru Renga-Ya

SERVES 4
PREPARATION TIME: 5 MINUTES

4 oz. (120 g) slice of raw,
sushi-quality salmon

1 tablespoon olive oil

Juice of ¼ lemon

1 pinch chives

Salt and pepper

Slice the salmon just before serving. Place the slices on very cold plates. Season with salt and a little freshly ground pepper. Drizzle the olive oil and lemon juice over and scatter the chives on the top.

Serve with hot toast. If you wish, add a spoonful of caviar to the center of each slice.

I took the inspiration for this recipe from Japanese cuisine.

Trout or Whiting Meunière
Truites ou merlans meunière

4 trout or whiting weighing
about 10 oz. (300 g) each

1 small bunch parsley

4 tablespoons flour

4 tablespoons (60 g) butter,
divided

1 tablespoon olive oil

2 cloves garlic, unpeeled

Salt and pepper

1 lemon

Ask the fish seller to clean the fish by removing the gills and cleaning without opening the stomach.

Carefully wash the parsley and remove the stems. Finely chop the parsley and set aside.

Salt and pepper the fish, then roll them in flour, and shake them to remove any excess before cooking.

Heat 2 tablespoons (30 g) of butter and the oil in a large frying pan. When it starts to foam, add the fish and garlic. Cook over high heat for about 6 minutes on each side, carefully turning them over once with a spatula (they should be browned on both sides).

Lift the fish out of the pan with a slotted spatula. Place them on a warm serving platter and sprinkle with parsley. Cut the lemon into quarters to garnish. Add the remaining butter to the frying pan, heat to melt, and pour over the fish. Serve immediately.

SERVES 4
PREPARATION TIME: 20 MINUTES
COOKING TIME: 30 MINUTES

Porgy Provençal
Daurade provençale au four

One 3 lb. (1.4 kg) porgy
or sea bream

1 small (50 g) onion

1 ¾ oz. (50 g) shallots

8 oz. (250 g) tomatoes

8 oz. (250 g) fresh mushrooms

2 tablespoons olive oil

Bouquet garni, made with
thyme, bay leaf, and parsley

⅓ cup (75 ml) dry white wine

Salt and pepper

1 lemon, quartered

Peel and finely slice the onion and shallot. Blanch the tomatoes to peel them easily; once peeled, cut them into quarters. Cut off any dirt from the stems of the mushrooms, then quickly dip the mushrooms in water with a little lemon juice squeezed in to wash them. Drain them and pat them dry; only slice the mushrooms right before use.

Preheat the oven to 350°F (180°C).

Scale and gut the fish, run it under cold water, and pat it dry using a clean towel. Brush the fish inside and out with a little oil, then place the bouquet garni inside it. Pour the remaining oil into a baking dish, add the fish, and surround it with the onion, shallot, tomatoes, and mushrooms. Salt and pepper, then pour in the white wine. Bake for 20 minutes. Turn off the oven, but leave the fish inside for 7 minutes more to finish cooking. Serve the fish in the dish it cooked in, garnished with lemon wedges.

Serving suggestions: Serve with rice or boiled potatoes.

Shellfish & Crustaceans

Lyon-Style Frogs' Legs
Grenouilles à la lyonnaise

SERVES 8 TO 10
PREPARATION TIME: 10 MINUTES
COOKING TIME: 15 MINUTES

50 large frogs' legs

2 onions

2 tablespoons (30 g) butter

2 tablespoons flour

1 tablespoon vinegar

Salt and freshly ground pepper

A few leaves parsley, chopped

Cut the onions into julienne slices and soften them in butter.

Dust the frogs' legs with flour and shake them well to remove any excess. Heat the butter in a pan until it sizzles and put the frogs' legs in. Sauté them over high heat until they brown slightly. Season with fine table salt and freshly ground pepper, and add the softened onions. Transfer to a serving platter.

When you are ready to serve, pour the vinegar into the burning hot pan and pour the liquid over the frogs' legs.

Sprinkle with chopped parsley.

Burgundy-Style Snails
Escargots à la bourguignonne

50 prepared snails plus their
shells

White bread crumbs

SPECIAL SNAIL BUTTER

⅓ oz. (10 g) garlic

1 oz. (30 g) shallot

⅔ oz. (20 g) parsley

2 ½ teaspoons (12 g) salt

6 turns of the pepper mill (2 g)

2 ¼ sticks (250 g) butter,
softened

Crush the garlic. Finely chop the shallots and the parsley. Add the three ingredients to the butter with the salt and pepper.

Combine thoroughly.

Preheat the oven to 425°F (210°C).

Place a knob of the prepared butter in each shell. If using canned snails, drain them. Then place a snail in each one; this will push the butter to the bottom of the shell. Close the shell by adding a little more prepared butter.

Pour just a little water into an ovenproof dish and arrange the shells in it. Place the filled shells in this. Sprinkle a few white bread crumbs over each snail and cook in the oven for 8 minutes.

Serve straight from the oven.

SERVES 6
PREPARATION TIME: 30 MINUTES
COOKING TIME: 20 MINUTES

Bordeaux-Style Crayfish
Écrevisses à la bordelaise

24 freshwater crayfish
1 medium-sized carrot
1 onion
2 shallots
1 ⅓ sticks (150 g) unsalted butter, divided
1 sprig thyme
1 bay leaf
Scant ½ cup (100 ml) cognac
1 ¼ cups (300 ml) white wine
3 tablespoons tomato paste
1 sprig chervil
1 sprig tarragon
Salt

Wash the freshwater crayfish and remove any eggs.

Cut the carrot into tiny dice. Cut the onion and shallots into tiny dice. Stew these vegetables gently with 3 tablespoons (50 g) butter, the prepared crayfish, a pinch of salt, the thyme, and bay leaf. Then turn up the heat until the crayfish turn a bright red.

Pour in the cognac, white wine, and tomato paste. Cover with the lid and cook for 8 to 10 minutes, still over high heat. Transfer the crayfish to a serving dish and keep warm.

Reduce the sauce by half. Remove from the heat and add the remaining butter and a pinch each of chopped chervil and tarragon.

Pour the sauce over the crayfish.

Moules Marinière

4 quarts (4 liters) mussels, weighing about 6 lb. (2.8 kg)
4 new onions
2 stalks celery
1 small bunch parsley
5 tablespoons (75 g) butter
2 cups (500 ml) dry white wine
Pepper
Juice of ½ lemon

Mussels should be tightly closed or–if they are open–should close tightly when scraped or tapped with the blade of a knife; if they stay open, it means they are dead and could be dangerous if eaten (don't worry, however, if the mussels open and close after being cleaned: they are simply breathing).

Clean the mussels one by one, scraping off any barnacles or mud, and pulling out the little "beard" that protrudes from the shell. Wash the mussels under cold running water (don't let them sit in water), and place in a large bowl as they are cleaned. Once clean, they should be shiny.

Peel and slice the onions. Remove the tough outer fibers from the celery, wash, and dice the stalks. Wash the parsley, remove its stems, then coarsely chop the parsley on a cutting board. Melt the butter in a large pot, add the onions, the celery, and half the parsley. Cook until the vegetables just begin to brown. Pour in the wine, add a little pepper, and bring to a boil. Cover the pot and remove from the heat. Leave for 5 to 7 minutes before cooking the mussels.

Add the mussels and lemon juice to the pot, cover, and return to the stove over high heat. Keep an eye on the mussels: once each mussel has opened, remove it with a slotted spoon. Remove one shell from each mussel, then place them in a large serving bowl (discard any mussels that haven't opened).

Line a sieve with a piece of doubled-over cheesecloth and strain the mussels' cooking liquid into the bowl with the mussels. Sprinkle with the remaining parsley and serve immediately.

Note: Other small shellfish, such as clams, can be prepared in the same way.

SERVES 4
PREPARATION TIME: 40 MINUTES
COOKING TIME: 30 MINUTES

4 quarts (4 liters) mussels,
weighing about 6 lb. (2.8 kg)

4 medium new onions

2 shallots

6 baby carrots

5 tablespoons (75 g)
butter, divided

3 cups (750 ml) dry white wine

Salt and pepper

1 bunch parsley

4 tablespoons (25 g) flour

Generous ¾ cup (200 ml)
heavy cream

Mussels in Creamy White Wine Sauce
Moules au vin blanc

Peel the onions, shallots, and carrots, and coarsely chop them on a cutting board. Melt 3 ½ tablespoons (50 g) butter in a large pot. Add the onions, shallots, and carrots, and simmer for 15 minutes. Add 2 cups (500ml) of the wine, salt, a little pepper, and cook slowly for 7 more minutes.

Meanwhile, clean the mussels (see facing page for instructions for selecting and cleaning mussels).

Place the mussels in a second pot, add the rest of the wine and a little pepper, bring to a boil, and cover the pot. As the mussels open, lift them out of the pot with a slotted spoon and discard one shell from each one. Place the mussels in a bowl and keep warm while finishing preparing the sauce.

Line a sieve with a piece of doubled-over cheesecloth and strain the mussels' cooking liquid into the pot with the vegetables; taste for seasoning. Wash the parsley, remove its stems and coarsely chop the parsley on a cutting board. Set aside. Make a beurre manié by mixing the remaining 1 ½ tablespoons (25 g) softened butter with the flour with your fingers until smooth, then break it into pea-sized pieces.

Whisk the cream into the boiling sauce; then whisk in the pieces of beurre manié. When the sauce is creamy, sprinkle the parsley over the mussels, add the sauce, and serve immediately.

Note: Other small shellfish, such as clams, can be prepared in the same way.

SERVES 6
PREPARATION TIME: 10 MINUTES
COOKING TIME: 15 MINUTES

1 lb. (500 g) sea scallops
or bay scallops

Flour

4 tablespoons (60 g) butter

1 tablespoon lemon juice

⅓ cup (75 ml) white vermouth

Generous ¾ cup (200 ml) crème
fraîche or heavy cream

Salt and pepper

Scallop Fricassee with Cream Sauce
*Fricassée de coquilles Saint-Jacques
à la crème*

To ensure the freshness of the scallops, ask the fish seller not to remove their shells until the moment you buy them, or, better still, do it yourself. Carefully wash the scallops.

Season the scallops with salt and pepper, roll them in flour, and shake them lightly to remove any excess before cooking.

Heat the butter in a large enameled cast-iron frying pan. When very hot, add the scallops and cook over moderate heat for 4 to 6 minutes if using sea scallops, 2 to 3 minutes if using bay scallops. Shake the pan frequently and turn the scallops over halfway through cooking.

Pour the lemon juice over the scallops, stir in the vermouth, then pour over the cream, stirring to scrape any juices from the bottom of the pan into the sauce. Bring the cream just to a boil, add a little salt and pepper, and serve.

Serving suggestions: This is delicious with broccoli.

Meat

Pepper Steaks
Steaks au poivre

SERVES 4
PREPARATION TIME: 7 MINUTES
COOKING TIME: 15 MINUTES

2 steaks from the tenderloin,
weighing 10 oz. (300 g) each

2 tablespoons (15 g)
whole peppercorns

2 tablespoons (30 g) butter

1 teaspoon Dijon mustard

6 tablespoons (100 ml) crème
fraîche or heavy cream

Salt

One hour ahead of time, take the steaks out of the refrigerator.

Place the peppercorns on a cutting board or table and coarsely crush them with a rolling pin. Lightly salt the steaks, then roll them in the peppercorns, pressing down on them as you do so. Leave for 15 minutes before cooking.

Heat the butter in a large frying pan until very hot, add the steaks, and cook over high heat 5 or 6 minutes on each side, then lift them out of the pan and keep warm on a serving platter while making the sauce.

Remove the pan from the heat, stir in the mustard and the cream, scraping the bottom of the pan to dissolve any meat juices, then place the pan back over the heat just long enough to heat the sauce (don't allow to boil). Add a little salt if needed, then pour over the meat and serve.

Serving suggestions: Serve with sautéed potatoes.

SERVES 4 TO 6
PREPARATION TIME: 10 MINUTES
COOKING TIME: 40 TO
45 MINUTES (15 MINUTES PER LB.)

A 2 ¼ lb. (1 kg) boned shoulder of lamb (weight without bone)

2 cloves garlic

2 tablespoons (30 g) softened butter

Salt and pepper

Roasted Lamb Shoulder
Épaule d'agneau à la broche

Two hours ahead of time, take the meat out of the refrigerator.

Peel the garlic and cut each clove into three wedges. Use a small knife to make six incisions in the meat and slide a wedge of garlic into each one. Salt and pepper the meat generously. Roll and tie into a sausage-like shape if the butcher hasn't already done so.

Roast the lamb on a spit if possible (see Note). Use a stove-top rotisserie or the spit attachment to your oven if it comes with one. Preheat to 425°F (210°C) for about 15 minutes, then spit the lamb, set it into place, pour a generous ½ cup (150 ml) of warm water into the drippings pan under the meat, and roast for 15 minutes per pound. Turn off the heating unit and leave the lamb turning on the spit 5 to 7 minutes more before making the sauce and serving (the meat will be very rare, as it should be).

To serve, remove the meat from the spit, place on a cutting board, and slice, being careful not to lose any of the juices that come out of the meat. Place the meat on a warm platter. Add the meat juices as well as 6 tablespoons (100 ml) of water to the roasting pan and bring to a boil, scraping the bottom of the pan to dissolve anything stuck to it. Break the softened butter into pieces. Stir in the butter, salt and pepper lightly, then pour the sauce into a sauceboat to serve on the side. Serve immediately.

Note: If you don't have a rotisserie, cook the lamb in the oven. Preheat the oven to 425°F (210°C), place the lamb in a roasting pan, and roast for 15 minutes per pound. Turn off the oven but leave the lamb inside for 7 minutes, then carve and make the sauce as described above, but in this case, add ½ cup (120 ml) water to the roasting pan before adding the butter.

SERVES 4
PREPARATION TIME: 20 MINUTES
COOKING TIME:
1 HOUR 30 MINUTES

1 milk-fed veal shank,
about 3 ½ lb. (1.5 kg)

5 ½ tablespoons (80 g) butter

1 large onion

9 oz. (250 g) new carrots

2 ripe tomatoes

Scant ½ cup (100 ml)
dry white wine

¾ cup (200 ml) veal stock

1 small bouquet garni

Salt and pepper

Braised Veal Shank
Jarret de veau à la ménagère

Season the veal shank with salt and pepper. Preferably using an oval ovenproof pot, color the veal on all sides in butter. While it is browning, cut the onion into large dice, the carrots into slices, and peel and chop the tomatoes. Add the diced onion and carrot slices and let them sauté a little. Then soften the chopped tomatoes.

Pour in the dry white wine and veal stock. Add the bouquet garni and cover with the lid. Either cook in a 350°F (180°C) oven, or over low heat for about 2 hours. Remove the bouquet garni just before serving.

Serve the veal shank in a deep dish surrounded by the vegetables and drizzled with the pan juices.

Serving suggestions: This hearty family dish is excellent accompanied by fresh pasta with butter.

SERVES 4
PREPARATION TIME: 15 MINUTES
COOKING TIME: 15 TO
20 MINUTES

4 veal cutlets weighing about
7-9 oz. (200-250 g) each

6 medium (150g) button
mushrooms

Juice of ¼ lemon

4 tablespoons (60 g)
butter, divided

Generous ½ cup (150 ml)
dry white wine (preferably
Pouilly-Fuissé)

6 tablespoons (100 ml) crème
fraîche or heavy cream

Salt and pepper

Veal Cutlets with Cream Sauce
Côtes de veau

About 90 minutes ahead of time, take the meat out of the refrigerator. Wash the mushrooms in water with a little lemon juice squeezed in.

Melt 1 ⅓ tablespoons (20 g) of butter in a small frying pan, then add the mushrooms and cook slowly until they soften; season with salt and pepper, and reserve.

In a large frying pan, melt the remaining butter. Salt and pepper the cutlets, then place them in the pan when the butter starts to foam. Cook over moderately high heat for 7 to 8 minutes on a side, then remove from the pan and keep warm while making the sauce.

Pour the wine into the pan the veal cooked in, stirring over high heat to detach any meat juices stuck to it, then add the mushrooms, cream, and salt and pepper as needed. Heat the sauce to boiling, pour immediately over the veal, and serve.

Serving suggestions: Serve with Spinach (see p. 172).

SERVES 6 TO 8
PREPARATION TIME: 20 MINUTES
COOKING TIME:
1 HOUR 30 MINUTES

1 lb. (500 g) neck (UK: scrag end) of veal

1 lb. (500 g) breast of veal

About 3 cups (750 ml) water

3 carrots

12 baby onions

Bouquet garni, made with 2 stalks celery, 1 sprig thyme, and ¼ bay leaf tied together

3 peppercorns

1 tablespoon (15 g) kosher salt

4 tablespoons (60 g) butter

2 tablespoons (12 g) flour

2 egg yolks

6 tablespoons (100 ml) whipping cream

1 tablespoon lemon juice

Pepper

Chopped parsley to garnish

Veal Blanquette
Blanquette de veau

Cut the veal into pieces about the size of an egg. Place in a pot, add the water (the meat should be almost, but not quite, covered by the water), and bring to a boil, skimming off any foam that rises. Peel the carrots, rinse them and cut them into thick sticks. Peel the onions and leave them whole. Remove the tough outer fibers of the celery, then tie together the celery, thyme, and bay leaf. As soon as the water comes to a boil, add the bouquet garni, along with the carrots, onions, peppercorns, and salt. Cover the pot, lower the heat, and simmer slowly for 1 hour.

Lift the meat and vegetables out of the pot with a slotted spoon, place in a serving dish, and keep warm while making the sauce. Discard the bouquet garni.

In a saucepan, melt the butter, then stir in the flour. When the mixture is smooth (do not allow to color), add the cooking liquid from the veal, little by little, whisking constantly. Once all the liquid has been added, bring to a boil and boil rapidly for 2 to 3 minutes to thicken the sauce, then remove the pot from the heat.

In a mixing bowl, whisk together the egg yolks and cream. Ladle in a little of the hot sauce, whisking constantly. Add the lemon juice, then pour back into the pot, stirring constantly. The sauce should be very hot but not boiling. Add a little pepper, pour the sauce over the meat and vegetables, sprinkle with chopped parsley, and serve immediately.

SERVES 4 TO 6
PREPARATION TIME: 20 MINUTES
COOKING TIME: AT LEAST
3 HOURS

2 ¼ lb. (1 kg) rump roast

About 4 oz. (125 g) fatback
(for larding)

½ calf's foot

9 oz. (250 g) salt pork

6 carrots

6 small onions

Bouquet garni, made with
3 sprigs parsley, 1 sprig thyme,
and ¼ bay leaf

4 tablespoons (60 g) butter

2 cups (500 ml) dry white wine

Generous ¾ cup (200 ml)
hot water

Salt and pepper

Family-Style Braised Beef
Boeuf mode

About 90 minutes ahead of time, take the meat out of the refrigerator. Lard the beef with strips of fatback, using a larding pin (or ask your butcher to do it). Salt and pepper the meat and calf's foot. Remove the rind from the salt pork and cut the salt pork into ½-in. (1-cm) cubes.

Peel the carrots, rinse them quickly and dry them. Cut them into sticks of roughly 2 in. (5 cm). Peel the onions and leave them whole. Carefully wash the parsley, then tie together the thyme, bay leaf, and parsley with twine.

In a large stew pot, preferably enameled cast-iron, melt the butter. When it starts to foam, add the onions and salt pork, and brown over high heat, stirring frequently. Add the beef and calf's foot, brown on all sides, then add the carrots, bouquet garni, and wine. Simmer uncovered for 1 hour, during which time some of the wine should evaporate. Add the water, salt, and pepper. Turn the meat over, bring to a boil, then cover the pot and simmer slowly for 2 hours (this dish must cook very slowly and for a long time).

To serve, discard the bouquet garni, then lift the meat and calf's foot out of the pot. Slice the meat and cut the foot into pieces, then place them on a hot platter, surrounded by the vegetables and salt pork. Use a spoon to skim off the fat on the surface of the cooking liquid, then pour the liquid over the meat and serve.

Variation: Leftovers are delicious eaten cold; in fact, some people always eat this dish cold rather than hot. Place the meat in a deep dish, arrange the carrots and onions around and on top, then strain the cooking liquid over it. Leave to cool, then refrigerate overnight.

Boiled Beef
Boeuf à la ficelle

SERVES 6
PREPARATION TIME: 15 MINUTES
COOKING TIME: 20 MINUTES

4 ½ lb. (2 kg) beef tenderloin or fillet of beef, trimmed

Just under 1 oz. (25 g) kosher salt

1 ¾ teaspoons (5 g) black peppercorns

1 onion, studded with 3 cloves

1 sprig parsley

1 sprig chervil

1 sprig tarragon

6 leeks, white part only

2 celery hearts (tender part of innermost ribs)

3 tomatoes

7 oz. (200 g) carrots and turnips, cut into sticks

Croutons

Grated Gruyère

Pour 13 cups (6 ⅓ pints/3 liters) of water into a large pot. Add the seasoning, the aromatic ingredients, and the vegetables. Bring to a boil and leave to boil for 5 minutes.

Tie a length of string around the beef, drop the beef into the broth and tie the string to the pot handle so that you can remove it easily.

Skim the surface thoroughly and leave at a very gentle simmer. Allow, on average, 10 to 15 minutes per pound (500 g) of meat, as you would for a roast beef; it should be pinky-red when you cut it.

Serve the fillet of beef surrounded by the vegetables.

Add a little butter to the broth and serve it with small croutons and grated Gruyère.

Serving suggestions: This dish is excellent accompanied by Tomato Sauce (see p. 53) flavored with tarragon and chives. Alternatively, you can simply serve the fillet with kosher salt, gherkins, and small pickled onions. A remoulade sauce is another possible accompaniment; this is a mayonnaise-based sauce containing mixed herbs, finely chopped gherkins, and capers, that is often served as an accompaniment to meat or seafood dishes.

Note: Thinly sliced fillet of beef, rib of beef, and leg of lamb may all be prepared using this method.

Roasted Beef Fillet
Filet de boeuf rôti

About 3 lb. (1.5 kg) beef fillet

3 ½ tablespoons (50 g) butter

Salt and pepper

Ask your butcher to bard the meat. Its juice will be tastier.

Take the meat out of the refrigerator about 2 hours before cooking.

Preheat the oven to 425°F (210°C).

On a cutting board, season the meat with salt and ground pepper, then place it in an ovenproof dish. Put the dish in the oven.

One minute before the end of the cooking time, take off the bard to allow all the surfaces of the roast to brown, and begin heating the serving platter, the plates, and the sauceboat.

At the end of the cooking time, switch off the oven but leave the roast inside for about another 5 minutes, so that the meat can rest. This will make it more tender and easier to cut.

Take the roast out of the oven, carve on a cutting board, and arrange on the serving platter. Keep the meat warm.

Discard any excess fat in the cooking dish, then heat the dish on a stove. Add juice collected from the carved meat as well as the butter cut into pieces. Also add half a ladleful of hot water, and salt and ground pepper. When the juice is frothy, pour it into the sauceboat.

Serve hot, accompanied by a gratin dauphinois and a watercress salad.

Note: If you have any roast fillet left over, you can serve it cold the next day, garnished with pickles, olives, and assorted mustards.

Veal and Olives
Rôti de veau

SERVES 4
PREPARATION TIME: 10 MINUTES
COOKING TIME: ABOUT 1 HOUR

1 ¾ lb. (800 g) veal rump roast

4 oz. (125 g) veal breast or tail, cut into pieces

1 onion

2 medium-sized ripe tomatoes

4 tablespoons (60 g) butter

1 generous cup (200 g) pitted green olives

Salt

One hour ahead of time, take the meat out of the refrigerator.

Peel and slice the onion. Blanch and peel the tomatoes, then cut them into quarters. Set aside.

Cut off any large pieces of fat from the veal. In a cast-iron pot just large enough for the meat, place the scraps of fat, along with the pieces of veal breast or tail, and brown lightly. Add the butter; when it has melted, add the onions and the veal roast. Cook to brown the meat evenly over moderate heat for 5 to 10 minutes, then add the tomatoes and stir to detach any meat juices stuck to the bottom of the pot. Salt lightly, cover the pot, place over low heat, and simmer for 40 minutes, turning the meat several times as it cooks.

While the meat is cooking, desalt the olives in a bowl of cold water; change the water once or twice.

After 40 minutes, lift the meat out of the pot and place it on a plate. Strain the contents of the pot into a mixing bowl, pressing on the meat and vegetables in the strainer to extract all of their juices. Place the strained liquid back in the pot, add the meat, drain the olives, and add them as well, then cover and simmer 20 minutes longer.

To serve, lift the meat out of the pot and place on a warm platter, surrounded by the olives and accompanied by mashed potatoes. Serve the sauce in a sauceboat on the side.

SERVES 4
PREPARATION TIME: 20 MINUTES
COOKING TIME:
1 HOUR 30 MINUTES

2 ¾ lb. (1.2 kg) boneless blade
or pork loin roast

8 baby onions

1 shallot

Generous ¾ cup (200 g) Dijon
mustard

About 6 oz. (175 g) pig's caul
(lace fat) or thinly sliced fatty
bacon

Generous ½ cup (150 ml) dry
white wine

⅓ cup (75 ml) hot water

Salt and pepper

Roasted Pork with Mustard
Rôti de porc à la moutarde

At least one hour ahead of time, take the meat out of the refrigerator.

Preheat the oven to 425°F (210°C).

Peel the onions and shallot, and set aside. Use a small spoon to spread the mustard all over the pork roast, then spread out the lace fat and completely wrap the pork up in it (if using slices of bacon, tie them around the roast from end to end). Tie off both ends of the lace fat, then tie two strings around the roast to hold the fat in place. Place the meat in a roasting pan, surround with the onions and shallot. Season with salt and pepper, add the white wine, and place in the oven. Once the roast begins to brown, baste it every 10 or 15 minutes. Cook for a total of 1 ¼ to 1 ½ hours, then turn off the oven but leave the roast inside for an additional 10 minutes.

Lift the roast out and place on a warm serving platter; place the roasting pan on top of the stove and boil the pan juices over high heat, add the hot water and a little pepper, boil rapidly for about 10 seconds, then pour into a sauceboat and serve with the meat.

Serving suggestions: Serve with a potato gratin or a split pea purée.

Veal Medallions with Softened Onions
Médaillons de veau à la compote d'oignons

SERVES 8
PREPARATION TIME: 20 MINUTES
COOKING TIME: 30 MINUTES

8 slices of veal, about 5-6 oz. (160 g) apiece, cut from the filet mignon into ½ in. (1-cm) thick medallions

Flour for dusting

1 stick plus 2 tablespoons (150 g) butter, plus extra for the truffles

Scant ¼ cup (50 ml) Madeira wine

Scant ½ cup (100 ml) dry white wine

3 cups (750 ml) crème fraîche or heavy cream

1 oz. (30 g) black truffles, cut into julienne strips

Salt and pepper

SOFTENED ONIONS

3 ½ lb. (1.5 kg) white onions

7 tablespoons (100 g) butter

2 tablespoons (30 ml) wine vinegar

Scant ½ cup (100 ml) cream

Salt and pepper

Season the medallions of veal with salt and pepper and dust them lightly with flour. In a low-sided, heavy-bottomed pot, melt the butter and sauté the veal, ensuring the slices remain tender.

When they are just done (they should be ever so lightly browned), arrange them on a serving platter. Cover them with buttered parchment paper and keep warm.

Deglaze the pot with the Madeira and white wine. Reduce by three-quarters. Add the cream and reduce again until the consistency is creamy and thick. Then adjust the seasoning.

Lastly, stew the julienned truffles lightly in butter (particularly important if they are raw) and incorporate them into the sauce.

Softened onions

Finely chop the onions. Stew them in a pot with the butter and season lightly with salt and pepper, taking care that they do not brown. When they are half cooked, add the vinegar. Leave to cook for a few moments and then stir in the cream until thoroughly incorporated. Cover the pot with the lid to finish cooking.

To serve, place a spoonful of onions beneath each medallion of veal; pour over the delicious sauce.

Alternatively, you can present the medallions individually in plates; this method allows them to be served hotter.

SERVES 6
PREPARATION TIME: 40 MINUTES
COOKING TIME: 40 MINUTES

Tournedos Clamart

6 tournedos,
3 ½ oz. (100 g) apiece

6 individual savory tartlet shells

3 large oven-baked potatoes

7 tablespoons (100 g) butter,
divided

1 lb. (500 g) peas cooked
à la française, braised in butter
with lettuce and baby onions

2 tablespoons oil

Scant ½ cup (100 ml) sherry

¾ cup (200 ml) veal *jus*

Salt and pepper

Prebake the tartlet shells: line them with parchment paper and fill with baking beans so that they retain their shape. Set aside.

Halve the baked potatoes and extract the flesh. In a bowl, season it with salt and pepper. Incorporate 3 tablespoons (50 g) butter using a fork to mash it in. Take the mashed potatoes and fashion six disks the size of the tournedos. Brown them in the oil. Carefully turn them over with a spatula to brown the other side. Arrange them in a circle on a round platter and keep warm.

Cook the tournedos for about 5 minutes on each side. Place one on each potato disk.

Arrange the pre-baked pastry shells around the tournedos. Place a spoonful of buttered peas in each tartlet.

Deglaze the sauté pan in which you have cooked the tournedos with the sherry and veal *jus*. Reduce it by two-thirds. Remove from the heat and add the remaining butter; transfer to a sauce dish. Do not pour this sauce into the serving platter as it would soften the potato disks.

It is the peas that give this dish its name: Clamart, not far from Paris, was famous for its peas and supplied them to the French royal court and to the city.

SERVES 6 TO 8
PREPARATION TIME: 5 MINUTES
COOKING TIME: 50 TO
55 MINUTES (15 MINUTES PER LB.)

3 ½ lb. (1.6 kg) leg of lamb,
excess fat removed

14 cups (3 ½ liters) water

2 ½ tablespoons (40 g)
kosher salt

2 carrots

2 onions

1 bouquet garni, made
with 2 stalks celery,
1 bunch parsley, 1 sprig thyme
and ¼ bay leaf

3 peppercorns

English-Style Leg of Lamb
Gigot à l'anglaise

Two hours ahead of time, take the meat out of the refrigerator.

Bring the water to a boil with the salt in a pot large enough to hold the lamb comfortably. Peel the carrots, then cut them lengthwise into quarters. Peel and quarter the onions. Remove the tough outer fibers of the celery. Wash the parsley, then tie together the thyme, bay leaf, parsley and celery with twine. Add the carrots, onions, parsley, thyme, bay leaf, celery, and peppercorns to the pot. When the liquid is boiling rapidly, add the lamb and cook 15 minutes per pound at a very slow, even boil. Skim off any foam that rises. When the cooking time is up, remove the pot from the heat, but leave the lamb in the liquid an additional 10 minutes, then lift it out and carve into thick slices (they will be nice and rare). Sprinkle with salt and pepper, place on a hot platter, and serve.

Serving suggestions: Serve with Baked Potatoes with Tomatoes (see p. 180) and a green salad. Any leftovers are delicious served cold with pickled gherkins and mustard. This dish can be livened up with an Aïoli Sauce (see p. 54) or Gribiche Sauce (see p. 50) served in a sauceboat on the side.

Boeuf Bourguignon

SERVES 4 TO 6
PREPARATION TIME: 20 MINUTES
COOKING TIME: 3 HOURS

2 ¼ lb. (1 kg) blade of beef

4 oz. (125 g) salt pork
or slab bacon

12 baby onions

About 4 carrots (1 lb./500g)

Bouquet garni, made with
2 stalks celery, 4 sprigs parsley,
1 sprig thyme,
and ¼ bay leaf

2 small cloves garlic

4 tablespoons (60 g) butter

1 tablespoon (6 g) flour

1 tablespoon tomato paste

1 bottle red wine

Salt and pepper

At least one hour and a half ahead of time, take the meat out of the refrigerator. Cut the meat into egg-sized pieces and the salt pork into ½ in. (1 cm) cubes.

Peel the onions and leave them whole. Peel the carrots, quickly run them under cold water, and cut them into sticks of roughly 2 in. (5 cm). Carefully wash the celery and parsley. Remove the tough outer fibers of the celery, then tie together the thyme, bay leaf, parsley, and celery. Peel and crush the garlic.

Melt the butter in a large cast-iron pot, add the onions and salt pork, and cook over moderate heat for 3 minutes, or until they begin to brown. Salt and pepper the meat, then add it to the pot and brown over high heat on all sides. Lower the heat, add the carrots and the bouquet garni, cover, and simmer for about 30 minutes; then lift the meat and bacon out of the pot with a slotted spoon and keep them warm. Stir the flour into the pot and heat until it starts to color. Stir in the tomato paste, then add the wine little by little, stirring constantly. Check the seasoning, add the garlic, and bring to a boil, stirring constantly. Return the meat and bacon to the pot, cover, and simmer for 2 ½ hours. Remove the bouquet garni, then serve the stew in its cooking pot.

Serving suggestions: Serve with steamed potatoes or a Potato Crêpe (see p. 162).

Tripe Sausage
Andouillettes

SERVES 4
PREPARATION TIME: 10 MINUTES
COOKING TIME: 1 HOUR

4 andouillettes (French
tripe sausages)

2 shallots

3 ½ tablespoons (50g) butter

2 tablespoons bread crumbs
(preferably white; see Note)

1 ¼ cups (300 ml) dry white wine

1 small bunch parsley

6 tablespoons (100 ml)
hot water

Salt and pepper

Preheat the oven to 350°F (180°C).

Peel and roughly chop the shallots. Set aside.

Melt the butter in a small roasting pan, add the sausages, and place in the oven for at least 45 minutes, turning over every 10 to 15 minutes.

Lift the sausages out of the pan and set them aside on a plate. Add the shallots, bread crumbs, salt, and pepper to the pan, stir in the white wine, heat to simmering on top of the stove, then place the sausages back in the pan and cook in the oven 15 minutes more. Turn off the oven but leave the sausages inside for another 10 minutes.

Remove the stems of the parsley, carefully wash the leaves, then coarsely chop.

To serve, remove the sausages from the pan and either slice them on a cutting board or leave them whole. Keep warm on a hot serving platter while making the sauce.

Place the roasting pan on top of the stove over high heat. Add the hot water, and boil, whisking, until the sauce is nice and creamy, then pour over the sausages, sprinkle with the parsley, and serve.

Note: White bread crumbs can be made by pulverizing stale white bread in a mortar or heavy-duty blender, but shop-bought bread crumbs may be used instead. The sauce will simply be brown instead of white.

Braised Mutton Shoulder with Turnips
Épaule de mouton braisée aux navets

SERVES 4 TO 6
PREPARATION TIME: 20 MINUTES
COOKING TIME:
2 HOURS 45 MINUTES

1 shoulder of mutton,
boned and trussed

3 tablespoons (50 g) butter

15 small onions

1 lb. (500 g) turnips

1 pinch sugar

⅔ cup (150 ml) dry white wine

2 cups (500 ml) low-salt broth

1 bouquet garni

1 clove garlic

Heat the butter in an oval Dutch oven. Gently brown the onions. While they are cooking, peel the turnips, quarter them, and trim them so that they are shaped like large walnuts. When the onions are done, remove them from the Dutch oven and replace them with the turnips. Sprinkle with a pinch of sugar and cook until colored. Set them aside with the onions.

Preheat the oven to 425°F (210°C).

Brown the mutton shoulder in the pot and pour in the white wine. When it is almost completely reduced, pour in enough broth to cover three-quarters of the mutton shoulder. Add the bouquet garni and bring to a boil. Cover with the lid and transfer to the oven. Cook for 2 hours.

Spoon the braising liquid over the meat, increasing the frequency as the liquid reduces.

After 2 hours, place the onions and turnips in the dish around the meat. If there is no longer sufficient liquid, add a little broth or water (this prevents the braising liquid becoming too salty).

Leave to simmer for an additional 25 to 30 minutes with the lid on, frequently spooning over the braising liquid.

Serve the shoulder of mutton in a deep dish surrounded by the vegetables. Pour over just the quantity of liquid you will need to serve your guests.

SERVES 4
PREPARATION TIME: 10 MINUTES
COOKING TIME:
ABOUT 25 MINUTES,
ACCORDING TO TASTE

1 boneless rib steak
weighing 1 ¾ lb. (800 g)

3 shallots

1 medium onion

1 anchovy fillet in oil

3 ½ tablespoons (50 g) butter

Generous ½ cup (150 ml)
red wine

Salt and pepper

Steak with Red Wine Sauce
Entrecôtes vigneronnes

One hour ahead of time, take the meat out of the refrigerator. Cut off any excess fat from around the steak.

Peel the shallots and onion. Finely chop the shallots, onion, and anchovies, either by hand or in a food processor. Place all together in a bowl and reserve for making the sauce. Melt the butter in a large frying pan until very hot, salt and pepper the steak on both sides, then place it in the pan. Cook the steak for 6 minutes on each side over moderately high heat if you like it rare, 8 minutes on each side if you like it medium rare. When done, lift the meat out of the pan and keep warm while making the sauce.

Stir the chopped onion mixture into the pan and cook for about 5 minutes, or until the onions have softened and begun to brown. Stir in the wine, bring to a boil, and boil for 1 to 2 minutes, or until the sauce has thickened slightly; add salt and pepper if needed.

You can either serve the steak as it is on a hot platter and slice it at the table with the sauce in a sauceboat on the side, or slice the meat, strain the sauce, spoon a little onto each dinner plate, place the slices of steak on top, and serve with any extra sauce in a sauceboat.

SERVES 4
PREPARATION TIME: 5 MINUTES
COOKING TIME: 20 MINTUES

Sausage with White Wine
Saucisses au vin blanc

8 small pork sausages
1 onion
1 clove garlic
3 tablespoons (40 g) butter
Generous ½ cup (150 ml)
dry white wine
Salt and pepper

Peel the onion and garlic, and finely chop them separately.

Prick the sausages in several places to keep them from bursting open while cooking.

Melt the butter in a frying pan. When hot, add the sausages and onion, and brown over moderate heat for about 10 minutes. Add the garlic and white wine, stirring to detach any juices stuck to the bottom of the pan. Cook 5 to 8 minutes more, then lift the sausages out of the pan and keep warm on a plate.

Add a little warm water to the cooking liquids in the pan if there isn't enough left to make a light sauce. Bring to a boil, season with freshly ground pepper and a little salt, stir, then pour over the sausages and serve.

Serving suggestions: Serve with mashed potatoes or a split pea purée.

Poultry & Game

Pot-Roasted Chicken
Poulet cocotte

SERVES 4 TO 5
PREPARATION TIME: 30 MINUTES
SOAKING TIME: 1 HOUR
COOKING TIME: 40 MINUTES

2 thin slices salt pork or bacon

3 lb. (1.4 kg) broiling or frying chicken (reserve the liver and gizzard)

4 tablespoons (60 g) butter, divided

6 baby onions, peeled

2 ¼ lb. (1 kg) new potatoes

1 tablespoon olive oil

½ teaspoon thyme leaves

4 tablespoons (60 ml) boiling water

Salt and pepper

Remove the rind from the salt pork or bacon. Soak salt pork for an hour, then drain and pat dry with a clean cloth (bacon doesn't need to be soaked). Cover the thighs of the chicken with the salt pork or bacon (barding), and tie the slices in place with string or attach them with toothpicks.

Melt 2 tablespoons of butter in a pot (preferably cast-iron) slightly larger than the chicken, and add the chicken along with its liver and gizzard. Cook over low heat, turning frequently for even browning, for 20 minutes. Season with salt and pepper.

Peel the baby onions. Scrape the potatoes with a small kitchen knife, wash in cold water, then drain and pat dry with a cloth before cooking.

While the chicken is browning, heat 2 tablespoons of butter and the oil in a frying pan. Add the onions, potatoes, and thyme. Cook for 20 minutes, shaking the pan to brown the vegetables evenly. Season with salt and pepper (the chicken and vegetables should be done at about the same time). When the cooking time is up, lift the vegetables out of the pan with a slotted spoon, add them to the pot with the chicken, and continue cooking for 15 minutes.

To serve, lift the chicken out of the pot, and carve. Place on a hot platter and surround with the vegetables. Pour the boiling water into the pot that the chicken cooked in, bring to a boil, stirring constantly, season with salt and pepper if needed, and serve in a sauceboat on the side.

Note: This is ideally a dish for springtime, when new potatoes are in season.

Guinea Hen or Partridges with Cabbage
Pintade ou perdreaux au chou

SERVES 4
PREPARATION TIME: 25 MINUTES
COOKING TIME: 45 MINUTES
FOR GUINEA HEN,
35 MINUTES FOR PARTRIDGES

About 2 ½ lb. (1 kg) guinea hen
or 2 partridges (see Note)

1 green Savoy cabbage

3 carrots

5 ounces (150 g) salt pork
or bacon

Bouquet garni, made with
1 sprig fresh or 2 sprigs dried
thyme and ¼ bay leaf

2 thin slices fatty bacon
or salt pork

7 tablespoons (100 g) butter
(for the birds), divided

½ cup (120 ml) hot water

Salt and pepper

Preheat the oven to 350°F (180°C).

Cut out the base of the cabbage, then cut it into quarters. Wash it under hot running water and drain. Peel and wash the carrots, then cut them lengthwise into quarters. Remove the rind from the salt pork or bacon, and dice the meat. Boil the cabbage for 15 to 20 minutes in a large pot of lightly salted boiling water with the carrots, diced salt pork or bacon, and the bouquet garni. Drain in a colander. Discard the bouquet garni. Place the cabbage in a roasting pan in the oven to dry out for 10 minutes, then remove from the oven and reserve with the pork and carrots.

Clean the bird(s). If using freshly killed partridges, pluck them just before cooking. Remove the liver carefully so that the bile does not burst. Cover the thighs and breast of each bird with the slices of fatty salt pork or bacon and attach with kitchen string. Sprinkle generously with pepper, but salt lightly because of the pork.

Melt 4 tablespoons (60 g) of butter in a pot (preferably enameled cast-iron) large enough to hold the bird(s) comfortably, and cook for 10 minutes, turning frequently to brown evenly. Cover the pot and finish cooking for 20 to 25 minutes for the partridges, or 35 minutes for a guinea hen, turning from time to time. Remove the pot from the heat but leave the bird(s) inside, covered, for 5 minutes more.

Meanwhile, reheat the cabbage, carrots, and diced salt pork by sautéeing them together in a frying pan with 3 tablespoons of butter.

To serve, lift the bird(s) out of the pot, discard the fatty salt pork or bacon from the thighs and breast, and carve. Place on a hot platter, surrounded by the vegetables and diced salt pork, and keep warm. Pour any carving juices into the pot, add the hot water, bring to a boil, season with a little pepper, then pour the sauce into a sauceboat and serve.

Note: Two pigeons may be used instead of partridges, or a Rock Cornish game hen instead of the guinea hen.

Joannès Nandron's Truffled Bresse Hen in a Pouch
Poularde de Bresse truffée en vessie Joannès Nandron

SERVES 4
PREPARATION TIME: ABOUT 1 HOUR
SOAKING TIME: 2 HOURS
COOKING TIME: 2 HOURS 15 MINUTES

1 pork bladder, plus salt and vinegar for soaking

1 Bresse hen, weighing about 4 lb. (1.8 kg)

8 large truffle slices

4 ¼ oz. (120 g) ground veal

5 tablespoons (80 ml) heavy cream

2 oz. (50 g) carrots

2 oz. (50 g) turnips, turned

2 oz. (50 g) celeriac

2 oz. (50 g) peas

2 oz. (50 g) green beans

1 leek, white part only

22 ½ pints (10 liters) white chicken stock, preferably prepared with the giblets and bones from the hen

A little Madeira wine

Salt and pepper

Ahead of time, leave the pork bladder to soak in cold water with salt and a little vinegar for 2 hours, then pat dry.

Remove the central bone from the hen, but leave the thigh and wing bones. Slip the truffle slices between the skin and the meat, spreading them between the breast and thighs.

Make a veal mousse: place the ground veal in a bowl placed over a larger bowl filled with ice and beat in the cream to make a smooth paste. Season and set aside.

Cook all the vegetables, season them, and combine them, with the exception of the leek, with the veal mousse. Fill the cavity of the hen with the mixture, inserting the leek white in the center.

Bring a pot of 22 ½ pints (10 liters) chicken stock to a boil.

(Continued on page 143)

Sew the hen shut and truss it so that it regains its original shape. Turn the pork bladder inside out and place the stuffed hen inside with a pinch of salt, pepper, and a few tablespoons of Madeira wine. Close the bladder tightly with string so that it is perfectly hermetic. Place the enclosed hen in the pot of hot stock and leave it to poach gently, without allowing the liquid to boil, for about 1 hour 30 minutes.

Remove it from the pot and present it to the guests, taking it out of the bladder. To carve, separate the wings and thighs. Serve each guest with a slice of hen accompanied by the vegetable and veal mousse mixture used to stuff the hen.

Note: 2 oz. (50 g) diced truffles and foie gras as well as the liver from the hen may be added to the ingredients listed.

This is one of the signature dishes of Joannès Nandron, a starred Michelin chef in Lyon, and the first chef outside Paris to obtain the prestigious Meilleur Ouvrier de France award in 1949.

SERVES 12 TO 15
PREPARATION TIME: 45 MINUTES
SOAKING TIME: 2 HOURS
CHILLING TIME: 24 HOURS
COOKING TIME: 30 MINUTES

3 fine duck livers, each
1 ¼ lb. to 1 lb. 5 oz. (500-600 g)
(the livers should come from
specially fattened ducks)

SEASONING

2 teaspoons plus a scant
½ teaspoon (12 g) fine table salt

6 turns (2 g) of the pepper mill

A little freshly grated nutmeg

2 sheets (4 g) gelatin

⅔ cup (150 ml) port wine

Duck Foie Gras Terrine
Terrine de fois gras de canard au naturel

The seasoning of foie gras prior to cooking is all-important. Use your scales for maximum accuracy. Foie gras is best prepared a day ahead.

Soak the duck livers for 2 hours in warm water, no hotter than 98°F (37°C).

Dab them dry and use your hands to open them up.

Carefully remove any bile you may find (it is a dark greenish color). Then remove all the veins and nerves you can see.

Combine the spices to make the seasoning. Soften the gelatin sheets in cold water. When they are rubbery, wring out the water and place them in the port. Stir until just dissolved.

Place the livers in a terrine and season them with the spices. Pour over the port. Cover the terrine and chill for 24 hours.

The next day, preheat the oven to 350°F (180°C). Place the terrine in the oven and immediately switch off the heat. Cook for 30 minutes, until the core temperature reaches 104°F (40°C).

Leave to cool in a cool place, and then chill before serving.

Chicken Marengo
Poulet sauté à la Marengo

SERVES 6
PREPARATION TIME: 30 MINUTES
COOKING TIME: 50 MINUTES

1 chicken, weighing about
3 lb. 5 oz. (1.5 kg)

4 tablespoons (60 g)
butter, divided

1 clove garlic

⅓ cup (75 ml) dry white wine

⅔ cup (150 ml) Tomato Sauce
(see p. 53)

⅓ cup (75 ml) veal *jus*

12 mushrooms

6 small eggs

6 crayfish

6 slices bread

6 truffle slices

Juice of ¼ lemon

1 sprig parsley, chopped

Preheat the oven to 425°F (210°C).

Roast the chicken in an ovenproof dish with half the butter for 35 minutes. Remove the chicken. Crush the garlic clove and throw it into the hot dish just before deglazing.

Deglaze the dish with the dry white wine and reduce it by two-thirds. Then stir in the tomato sauce and veal *jus*. Carve the chicken roughly into six pieces and keep warm.

Put the carcass and thighs into the dish with the sauce and bring to a boil. Remove from the heat and incorporate some butter.

Sauté the caps of the mushrooms and set aside. Fry the eggs, one per person. Truss the crayfish by pinning the claws to the tail. Cook them in a court bouillon or sauté them in butter. Prepare the toast: cut the bread into heart shapes and brown the slices in butter. Cook the truffle slices in the sauce for 2 minutes at the last minute.

Arrange the chicken pieces on a serving dish and garnish them with the mushroom caps. Pour the sauce over. Then squeeze the lemon juice over the pieces and sprinkle with chopped parsley.

Chicken Liver Soufflé
Gâteaux aux foies de volaille

SERVES 4
PREPARATION TIME: 30 MINUTES
COOKING TIME: 45 MINUTES

At least 3 chicken livers, weighing about 4 ½ oz. (125 g)

2 ¼ lb. (1 kg) fresh tomatoes

1 tablespoon olive oil

Bouquet garni, made with 1 sprig fresh and 1 sprig dried thyme, ¼ bay leaf, and 1 stalk celery

1 teaspoon (5 g) granulated sugar

1 small onion (50g)

2 cups (500 ml) milk, plus milk for the onion

1 bunch parsley

1 clove garlic

3 ½ oz. (100 g) stale bread

4 eggs, separated

1 ½ tablespoon (20 g) butter

Salt and pepper

To make the fresh tomato sauce for this recipe, blanch and peel the tomatoes, cut them into wedges, and place in a saucepan with a teaspoon of olive oil and the bouquet garni. Add the sugar, bring to a boil, then lower the heat, and boil gently over moderate heat for about 40 minutes or until thick, stirring frequently. Season with salt and pepper. Just before serving, remove the bouquet garni and stir in the remaining olive oil.

Preheat the oven to 375°F (190°C). While the sauce is cooking, you can make the soufflé. If possible, buy livers that are light in color–they are the best. Peel and slice the onion. Place the slices in a saucepan, add enough cold milk to cover, bring just to a boil, then drain and set aside.

Carefully wash the parsley and remove its stems. Peel the garlic. Place the bread in a bowl and add the milk; once the bread has softened, crush it with the prongs of a fork, then pour off any excess milk. Place the bread on a cutting board with the livers, onions, garlic, and parsley, and chop to a paste using a food mill. Place in a mixing bowl, stir in the egg yolks, and season with salt and pepper.

Place the butter in a 7-in. (18-cm) soufflé mold and put it in the oven just long enough for the butter to melt. Remove from the oven and turn the dish to coat the sides with the butter.

Beat the egg whites until stiff and fold them into the liver mixture, then pour the mixture into the soufflé mold. Place in the oven and bake for 45 minutes (check for browning by looking through the window in the oven door, but don't open it until the soufflé is done). Serve the soufflé hot from the oven, with the tomato sauce in a sauceboat on the side.

SERVES 6
PREPARATION TIME: 15 MINUTES
COOKING TIME: 20 MINUTES

Quail with Grapes
Cailles aux raisins

6 quail

3 tablespoons (40 g) butter

1 large bunch very ripe
Chasselas (white) grapes

Scant ½ cup (100 ml) veal stock

Salt and pepper

Preheat the oven to 450°F–475°F (240°C).

Prepare the quails as for roasting. Heat the butter in an oven-proof earthenware lidded casserole dish, then add the quail.

Season with salt and pepper, brown quickly on all sides, then cover the pan and finish cooking in the very hot oven. These two steps should take about 12–15 minutes.

While the quail are cooking, peel the grapes and deseed them if necessary using a fine needle. Allow about eight grapes per quail.

When the quail are cooked, add the grapes to the casserole dish. Add the veal stock to deglaze the pan, then cover with the lid and bring to a quick boil.

Serve immediately in the casserole dish presented on a platter lined with a folded table napkin.

Stuffed Boiled Hen
Poularde farcie

SERVES 4 TO 6
PREPARATION TIME: 25 MINUTES
COOKING TIME: 2 HOURS TO
2 HOURS 30 MINUTES

5 lb. (2.2 kg) top-quality stewing
hen, giblets included

4 chicken livers

1 cup (50 g) fresh bread crumbs

½ cup (120 ml) milk

1 large clove garlic

2 shallots

1 small bunch parsley

3 ½ oz. (100 g) salt pork

2 eggs

4 to 6 medium carrots
(about 2 lb./1 kg)

2 onions

1 bunch celery

4 large leeks

1 sprig thyme

¼ bay leaf

1 clove

3 peppercorns

2 ½ tablespoons (40 g)
kosher salt

Salt and pepper

About one hour and a half ahead of time, take all of the ingredients out of the refrigerator.

First make the stuffing. Chop the chicken livers. Chop the hen's liver and heart, and set aside in a bowl with the other chopped livers. Place the crumbed bread in another bowl with the milk and leave for about 10 minutes, or until the bread has completely softened. Peel the garlic and the shallots, and carefully wash the parsley. Remove the rind from the salt pork and chop the salt pork. Place the garlic, shallots, parsley, and salt pork on a chopping board and roughly chop them all using a *mezzaluna* (herb chopper), or a blender. Use the prongs of a fork to crush the bread, then stir in the livers, shallots, garlic, parsley, salt pork, and eggs. Season generously with salt and pepper, use your hands to knead the stuffing, then stuff the hen and sew it up so that none of the stuffing will escape while cooking.

Peel the carrots and onions, and remove the tough outer fibers of the celery. Carefully wash the leeks. Tie together the leeks and celery with one piece of twine, and the thyme and bay leaf with another. Stick the clove in one of the onions.

Place the hen in a large pot with the thyme, bay leaf, peppercorns, and onion. Pour in about 14 cups (3 ½ liters) water, enough to cover completely, add the salt, and bring to a boil. Skim off any foam, then lower the heat, cover the pot, and simmer for 90 minutes. Add the leeks, carrots, and celery, and cook for another hour. To serve, remove the hen from the pot, carve, and serve on a hot platter with the stuffing and vegetables around it, and Dijon mustard and pickled gherkins on the side.

Note: If you like, the cooking liquid (bouillon) can be served first, as a soup, with slices of toasted country-style bread (any leftover bouillon can be used for other recipes).

Duck with Turnips
Canard aux navets

SERVES 4
PREPARATION TIME: 35 MINUTES
COOKING TIME: 40 MINUTES

3 lb. (1.4 kg) duck with liver, heart, and lungs

1 sprig parsley, leaves only

4 ½ oz. (125 g) salt pork

3 small shallots

3 duck or chicken livers

1 cup (40 g) coarsely crumbled dry or stale toast (or melba toast)

1 sprig thyme, leaves only

½ bay leaf, crushed

Salt and pepper

1 egg yolk

1 pinch four-spice mixture or allspice

2 lb. (900 g) turnips

Nutmeg

Generous ¾ cup (200 ml) crème fraîche or heavy cream

1 tablespoon cognac

5 teaspoons (25 g) softened butter, broken into 5 pieces, plus butter for pans

Prepare the duck for roasting and season; save the heart, liver, and lungs for the sauce. Preheat the oven to 425°F (210°C).

Wash the parsley, remove the stems and keep only the leaves.

Remove the rind from the salt pork. Peel the shallots, and roughly chop two shallots and the salt pork on a cutting board, along with the chicken livers. Add the toast, thyme, bay leaf, and parsley to the cutting board, and finely chop using a food mill. Add the egg yolk. Season with the four-spice mixture, then stuff the duck and sew it closed.

When the duck is ready to roast, prepare the turnips. Peel and slice them very thinly, blanch them for 2-3 minutes in lightly salted boiling water, then drain and cool under running water. Pat dry. Lightly butter a baking dish and arrange the turnip slices in an overlapping row. Season the first layer with salt, pepper, and nutmeg, then finish filling the dish. Spoon over the cream, season again, and set aside.

Place the duck in a lightly buttered roasting pan, add 4 table-spoons (60 ml) of water, and roast for a total of 50 minutes. After 30 minutes, place the turnips in the oven as well, and continue cooking for the final 20 minutes.

(Continued on page 154)

Chop the duck's liver, heart, and lungs to a paste along with the third shallot. Place in a small saucepan with the cognac, season, and cook over very low heat for 1 minute; remove from the heat.

When the duck is done, remove it from the oven and carve it on a cutting board, saving any juices. Remove the legs and thighs, and place them on aluminum foil, skin-side down; place them back in the oven to continue cooking while you finish off the dish.

Place the sliced duck breasts on a hot platter with the stuffing and keep warm. Discard almost all the fat in the roasting pan. Add the carving juices, the cognac-liver mixture, 5 tablespoons (750 ml) warm water, and the softened butter, and heat on top of the stove, stirring constantly. When the butter has melted, pour the sauce into a sauceboat.

Remove the legs from the oven, place on the serving platter with the breasts, and serve, with the turnips and sauce on the side.

SERVES 8
PREPARATION TIME: 15 MINUTES
COOKING TIME:
ABOUT 1 HOUR 30 MINUTES

5 ½ lb. (2.5 kg) capon
(see Note)

2 cups (250 g) black olives

2 ½ tablespoons (40 g) butter
(for the roasting pan)

½ cup (120 ml) warm water

3 ½ tablespoons (50 g)
softened butter

Salt and pepper

Roasted Capon with Black Olives
Chapon de Bresse rôti aux olives noires

At least two hours ahead of time, take the capon out of the refrigerator.

Preheat the oven to 450°F-475°F (240°C), or as high as it will go.

Rinse the olives in cold running water and drain. Place them inside the capon, then sew up the bird to keep them inside while roasting. Sprinkle the capon with salt and pepper, place it in a generously buttered roasting pan, and roast for 1 ½ hours (about 17 minutes per pound). Baste after the first 15 minutes and every so often thereafter. Once the cooking time is up, turn off the oven, but leave the bird inside for another 10 minutes before serving.

To serve, lift the capon out of the roasting pan and carve; save any juices that come from it for the sauce. Remove the olives and place in a bowl. Break the softened butter into 10 pieces. Add the warm water and any carving juices to the roasting pan, place over high heat, and add the softened butter. Bring to a boil, whisking constantly; when all the butter has melted, add salt and pepper, and pour into a sauceboat.

Serve with the sauce and the olives on the side.

Serving suggestions: Serve with sautéed potatoes or green beans.

Note: If a capon is unavailable, two 3 lb. (1.4 kg) chickens may be used instead. Follow the directions given here, but roast for only 50 minutes.

SERVES 4
PREPARATION TIME: 30 MINUTES
COOKING TIME: 50 MINUTES

3 lb. (1.4 kg) rabbit

1 tomato

5 oz. (150 g) salt pork or slab bacon

Bouquet garni, made with 1 sprig fresh or 2 sprigs dried thyme, ¼ bay leaf, and 2 sprigs parsley

4 shallots

9 oz. (250 g) fresh mushrooms

2 cloves garlic, whole and unpeeled

7 tablespoons (100 g) butter

Generous ½ cup (150 ml) dry white wine

Salt and pepper

Lyon-Style Rabbit
Lapin sauté à la lyonnaise

Ask your butcher to cut the rabbit into 10 pieces. Season.

Blanch and peel the tomato, and set aside. Remove the rind from the salt pork or slab bacon, and cut into ½-in. (1-cm) cubes. Tie the bouquet garni. Peel the shallots. Cut off the bottom of the mushrooms, wash them and cut them into quarters.

Melt 5 tablespoons (75 g) of butter in a large, high-sided frying pan. When it foams, add the rabbit, shallots, garlic, salt pork, and bouquet garni and cook for 10 minutes, turning frequently, to brown evenly. Cut the tomatoes into quarters, add to the pan and cook very slowly, uncovered, for 25 minutes, turning three to four times. While the rabbit is cooking, melt 2 tablespoons (30 g) of butter in a small frying pan, add the mushrooms, and sauté until all their moisture has evaporated and they begin to brown. Lift them out of the pan and add them to the rabbit.

After 25 minutes of cooking time for the rabbit, add the white wine, stirring to detach any meat juices, cover, and cook for 8 minutes more over very low heat. Taste for salt and pepper, then remove the pan from the heat and leave the rabbit 5 minutes longer in the pan. Place the rabbit in a hot serving dish, pour over the sauce, and serve.

SERVES 6 TO 8
MARINATING TIME: 6 HOURS
PREPARATION TIME: 30 MINUTES
COOKING TIME:
1 HOUR 40 MINUTES
CHILLING TIME: OVERNIGHT

2 ¾ lb. (1.25 kg) rabbit

1 lb. (500 g) pork jowl, cut into
8 to 10 pieces

Salt and pepper

3 carrots, peeled and quartered

Bouquet garni, made with
2 celery stalks, 1 sprig of thyme,
¼ bay leaf, and 3 sprigs parsley

5 peppercorns

1 tablespoon olive oil

1 bottle dry white wine

6 ½ tablespoons (100 g) lard

Rabbit Pâté
Rillettes de lapin

Ask your butcher to cut the rabbit into six pieces, at the joints so as not to splinter the bones. Place in a large bowl with the pork, salt, and pepper, then add the carrots, onions, and the bouquet garni. Stir in the peppercorns, oil, and wine, then leave to marinate for 6 hours, or overnight, before cooking.

Lift the rabbit and pork out of the marinade and pat dry with a clean cloth. Heat the lard in a large pot over moderate heat (the pot should be wide enough for all the meat to sit on the bottom without piling up). Cook the rabbit and pork for 10 minutes to brown lightly, turning frequently, then pour all the marinade ingredients into the pot (the liquid should barely cover the meat). Bring to a boil, then lower the heat and cook at a slow boil, uncovered, for about 1 ½ hours. Measure the liquid in the pot occasionally by straining it into a measuring cup; when the cooking is done, there should be 1 cup (250 ml) of liquid left.

Lift the rabbit and pork out of the pan. Use two forks to shred the meat (discard the bones) by holding the meat with one fork and pulling at it with the other fork. Place the shredded meat into a salad bowl. Strain the remaining cooking liquid, add to the meat, and season with salt and pepper. Refrigerate overnight in individual glass or earthenware pots before serving.

Serving suggestions: Serve with rustic bread, pickled gherkins, and a green salad.

Vegetables

Stuffed Tomatoes
Tomates farcies

SERVES 6
SOAKING TIME: OVERNIGHT
PREPARATION TIME: 40 MINUTES
COOKING TIME:
1 HOUR 30 MINUTES

7 oz. (200 g) salt pork

1 generous cup (300 g) leftover boiled beef or veal or pork

12 large tomatoes

1 sprig thyme

¼ bay leaf

4 small onions

1 cup (250 ml) milk

3 slices of dry toast or melba toast

1 small bunch parsley

1 clove garlic

1 egg

4 tablespoons (60 g) butter

Salt, pepper, and nutmeg

Soak the salt pork overnight in cold iced water (change the water several times). Once desalted, take the salt pork out and pat it dry. Place the salt pork in a saucepan, cover with cold water, bring to a boil, then lower the heat and simmer for about 1 hour. Drain and leave to cool before using.

One hour ahead of time, take all the ingredients out of the refrigerator. Wash the tomatoes, and cut off the top third of each one. Reserve the tops. Use a spoon to carefully scoop out the seeds and pulp, being careful not to puncture the skins. Reserve the pulp and seeds. Lightly salt the inside of each tomato. Preheat the oven to 350°F (180°C).

Place the seeds and pulp in a small saucepan with the thyme, bay leaf, salt, and pepper, and simmer for 15 to 20 minutes, stirring frequently. Reserve. While the sauce is cooking, peel and slice the onions. Place the onions in a saucepan with the milk, bring to a boil, then lower the heat and simmer for 7 to 8 minutes. Lift the onions out of the milk with a slotted spoon and chop them coarsely. Save the milk.

Crumble the toast. Place in a mixing bowl and add the onion milk. Soak for 10 minutes, then crush the toast with a fork; pour off any excess milk. Peel the garlic and chop the garlic and parsley leaves. Remove the rind from the salt pork and chop the salt pork and the leftover meat, and add it to the toast along with the onion, garlic, and parsley. All the ingredients for the stuffing can be worked through a meat grinder, if preferred. Don't grind too finely. Mix well, then add the egg, salt, pepper, and nutmeg, and knead with your hands to mix thoroughly.

(*Continued on page 162*)

Butter a baking dish just large enough to hold all the tomatoes. Fill each tomato with stuffing, add a piece of butter to each tomato, then put the top sections back in place and arrange them in the baking dish. Pour the tomato sauce made earlier into the dish around the tomatoes, then place in the oven and bake for 1 hour. Serve hot from the oven in the baking dish.

SERVES 4
PREPARATION TIME: 15 MINUTES
COOKING TIME: 15 TO 20 MINUTES

1 lb. (500 g) potatoes (do not use new potatoes)
1 egg
3 tablespoons olive oil
Salt and pepper

Potato Crêpe
Crique

Just before cooking, wash the potatoes, wipe them dry, and peel them (do *not* wash after peeling but wipe them off with a dry cloth if necessary). Grate the potatoes coarsely, place them in a bowl with the egg, salt, and pepper, and mix well.

Heat 2 tablespoons of the oil in a large frying pan (preferably cast-iron). When very hot, add all the grated potatoes and spread them out with the prongs of a fork, pressing down on them lightly to make a large crêpe, or pancake, of even thickness. Cook over moderately high heat for 6 to 8 minutes, or until the underside has browned, then slide the crêpe out into a large plate.

Place 1 more tablespoon of oil in the pan, then place a second plate on top of the crêpe and turn the crêpe upside down. Lift off the first plate and slide the crêpe back into the pan to finish cooking 6 to 8 minutes on the second side. Serve immediately.

Serving suggestions: Serve as a garnish with meat, or as a light lunch, accompanied by a green salad flavored with a little garlic, if you like it, and a Vinaigrette (see p. 56) made with olive oil and seasoned with finely chopped fresh herbs (parsley, chervil, chives, tarragon, etc.), depending on what's in season.

Potato Croquettes
Croquettes de pommes de terre

SERVES 4
PREPARATION TIME: 20 MINUTES
COOKING TIME: 35 MINUTES

1 lb. (500 g) potatoes
7 tablespoons (100 g) butter
4 egg yolks
1 pinch freshly grated nutmeg
2 tablespoons flour
1 egg
1 tablespoon olive oil
2 tablespoons bread crumbs
Oil for frying
Salt and pepper

Peel the potatoes and cook them in gently simmering salted water until their flesh gives way to pressure. Do not wait until they are so well cooked that they burst or fall apart.

Drain them well and return them to the cooking pot; leave it on the corner of the burner or over minimal heat so that their water evaporates.

Turn them into a sieve and press them through using a potato ricer. Be careful to use pressure on the ricer and not rotate it, as this would cause the mashed potato to become elastic.

Put the hot mashed potato in a pot and, with a spatula or wooden spoon, work in the butter energetically. The potatoes will become white; now incorporate the egg yolks and nutmeg. Check to see if the mixture is sufficiently salted and leave to cool.

Prepare a working surface very lightly dusted with flour. Divide the mashed potato into several parts and roll each one out into a log shape. Cut the logs into shapes the size of a slightly elongated cork.

Beat the whole egg with a small pinch of salt and olive oil. Dip the potato "corks" into this mixture and then into the bread crumbs.

Heat an oil bath until it just begins to smoke. Drop the potato croquettes into the oil and fry until they are golden and crisp. Drain them on paper towel and sprinkle with just a little fine salt.

Fold a napkin on a plate and arrange a mound of croquettes on top.

Piemontaise Risotto
Risotto à la piémontaise

SERVES 4
PREPARATION TIME: 15 MINUTES
COOKING TIME: 20 MINUTES

1 heaped cup (9 oz./250 g) rice, preferably round grain

1 large onion

7 tablespoons (100 g) butter

2 cups (500 ml) white broth or stock

1 oz. (30 g) tablespoons grated Parmesan

Salt and pepper

Wash the rice and drain it well. Chop the onion very finely. Melt the butter in a pan and fry the onion very gently until it is translucent and barely begins to color. When it is completely softened, add the rice.

Stir the rice and onion, leaving the pan over very low heat. When you see that the grains of rice have absorbed the butter, pour in an amount of broth or stock equal to twice the volume of the rice.

Bring to a simmer and cover with a tight-fitting lid. When the rice is cooked, mix it through with a fork to separate the grains, check the seasoning, and stir in 2 tablespoons (30 g) butter and grated Parmesan (preferably) or Gruyère.

Paris-Style Gnocchi
Gnocchis à la parisienne

SERVES 4
PREPARATION TIME: 30 MINUTES
COOKING TIME: ABOUT 1 HOUR

OLD-FASHIONED GNOCCHI

1 cup (250 ml) milk

3 tablespoons (50 g) butter

1 pinch salt

1 pinch freshly grated nutmeg

1 ¼ cups (125 g) flour, sifted

3 eggs

Gnocchi dough

In a saucepan, bring the milk, butter, salt, and nutmeg to a boil. As soon as the butter melts, pour in the flour, mixing with a flexible spatula or wooden spoon as you do so. Move the saucepan to the corner of the burner or turn the heat to minimum, continuing to stir for 5 minutes. This will dry out the dough without burning it. Then remove from the heat altogether and stir in the eggs, one by one, until the dough is very smooth and not too thick.

Gnocchi

In a large, deep sauté pan, bring water to a boil, adding 1 ¾ teaspoons salt (8 g) for every 4 cups (1 liter). Leave the water simmering over very low heat.

(*Continued on page 169*)

Spoon the dough into a pastry bag fitted with a plain, medium tip, and with your left hand press it out over the simmering water. With your right hand, cut it into pieces 1 ½ in. (4 cm) long as they are extruded from the tip, using a knife dipped frequently into hot water. Alternatively, you can take a walnut-sized piece of dough with a teaspoon dipped into hot water (you must dip it each time) and slip it into the poaching water. Return the pan to the heat and leave to boil for 1 minute. Then turn down the heat or move the pan to the side of the burner and leave to simmer gently for 15 minutes. Gradually, the gnocchi will rise to the surface as they finish poaching. Drain one of them and test for doneness by pressing lightly–it should have some elasticity. Remove the gnocchi with a slotted spoon and drain them on a clean cloth.

Mornay sauce

MORNAY SAUCE

2 cups (500 ml) Béchamel or White Sauce (see p. 54)

Scant ½ cup (2 oz./50 g) grated Gruyère cheese

2 egg yolks

3 tablespoons cream

2 tablespoons (30 g) butter, divided

Bring the béchamel (white) sauce to a boil. Stir in the grated Gruyère and leave to simmer, stirring constantly, until the cheese has completely melted. Immediately remove from the heat (the sauce should not boil any longer) and whisk in the egg yolks together with 1 tablespoon of cream. This will thicken the sauce. If you do not have cream, use milk. Return to the heat and reheat gently, whisking briskly all the time, until it is about to start boiling. Remove from the heat and stir in the remaining cream and 1 ½ tablespoons butter.

⅔ oz. (20 g) pale bread crumbs

1 scant cup (3 ½ oz./100 g) grated Gruyère cheese

Preheat the oven to 350°F (180°C). Spread a few spoonfuls of Mornay sauce on the bottom of an ovenproof dish. Arrange a layer of old-fashioned gnocchi on top, and pour over a generous serving of the Mornay sauce.

Combine the bread crumbs with the grated cheese and sprinkle the mixture over the gnocchi. Melt the remaining butter and drizzle it over the top. Place in the oven and cook for about 25 minutes, until a nice crust forms. The gnocchi will triple in volume as they cook. Serve very hot.

Artichokes with Various Sauces
Artichauts avec sauces diverses

SERVES 4
PREPARATION TIME: 10 MINUTES
COOKING TIME: 10 MINUTES

4 globe artichokes
1 pinch parsley or chervil
Salt

Cut the artichoke stems at the base of the leaves. Using a pair of scissors, cut off the tips of the outside leaves and trim off the top third. Wash the artichokes and tie them so that the leaves stay in place while they boil. Prepare a pot of boiling water and place the artichokes in it. Leave them to cook for 10 minutes and drain the water off.

Place them in a fresh pot of boiling water, add salt, and cook at a good boil. To check for doneness, press lightly on the bottom of an artichoke. If it gives way easily, or you can easily detach one of the outside leaves, they are done.

To serve hot:
Drain the artichokes and place them upside down over a dish-cloth or towel. Serve them accompanied by a bowl of melted butter, Hollandaise Sauce (see p. 57), mousseline sauce, cream sauce, Béchamel or White Sauce (see p. 54), and so on.

To serve cold:
Allow the artichokes to drain and cool upside down. Remove the central leaves from the artichokes and set them aside. Then scrape out the fuzzy choke. Take the central leaves and put them, tips inside, into the artichoke. Place the chopped parsley or chervil within the little bowl shape formed by the bottom of the leaves. Accompany with a cold sauce, such as a Vinaigrette (see p. 56), light mayonnaise, with or without mustard, sauce tartare, and so on.

Note: To eat, pull off each leaf and dip the fleshy end in the dressing before scraping off the flesh between your teeth. Discard the rest of the leaf.

SERVES 4
PREPARATION TIME: 15 MINUTES
COOKING TIME: 10 MINUTES

Spinach
Épinards

3 ½ lb. (1.5 kg) fresh spinach

1 generous tablespoon (30 g) kosher salt

1 medium onion

3 tablespoons (50 g) butter

6 tablespoons (100 ml) crème fraîche or heavy cream

Salt and pepper

Bring 14 cups (3 ½ liters) water and the salt to a boil in a large pot.

While the water is heating up, carefully clean the spinach: remove the stem and thick rib from each leaf, then wash in several changes of cold water. Carefully drain after washing, then drop the spinach little by little into the boiling water, pushing each addition into the water with a slotted spoon before adding more. Boil for 5 minutes from the time the water comes back to a boil (if you don't have a pot large enough to cook all the spinach at once, cook only as much as you can, remove from the pot with a slotted spoon, drain, cool under running water, and leave in the colander while cooking the rest). When all the spinach is cooked, drain in a colander, cool immediately under cold running water, then squeeze out the water with your hands, and reserve the spinach in a bowl.

Peel and slice the onion. Melt the butter in a high-sided frying pan, brown the onion lightly, then add the spinach, salt, and pepper, and stir over moderate heat with a wooden spoon to heat thoroughly. Add the cream, cook 5 minutes more, and serve immediately on a hot platter.

Serving suggestions: You can serve the spinach garnished with hard-boiled eggs cut in half and squares or triangles of bread fried in butter (croutons), for a nice effect.

Note: Fresh sorrel can be cooked in the same way.

SERVES 4
PREPARATION TIME: 15 MINUTES
COOKING TIME: 35 MINUTES

Cauliflower au Gratin
Gratin de chou-fleur

1 cauliflower, weighing about 2 lb. (900 g)

1 tablespoon olive oil

A stale breadcrust (optional)

2 ½ tablespoons (40 g) butter

1 cup (250 ml) milk

1 tablespoon (10 g) cornstarch

1 tablespoon water

6 tablespoons (100 ml) whipping cream

⅓ cup (50 g) grated Gruyère cheese

Nutmeg

Salt and pepper

Cut the central core from the cauliflower and separate the florets. Wash them carefully in cold water.

Bring lightly salted water to a boil and add the oil; you can also add a stale breadcrust to the water (it will absorb some of the odor of the cauliflower as it cooks). Add the cauliflower, boil for 5 minutes from the time the water comes back to a boil, then drain. Butter a baking dish (enameled cast-iron or porcelain), place the cauliflower in it, and reserve.

Preheat the oven to 350°F (180°C).

Heat the milk in a saucepan; while it's heating, mix the cornstarch and cold water together. Once the milk boils, remove the pot from the heat and stir in the cornstarch mixture. Return to the heat and bring to a boil, stirring constantly. Cook until the sauce is thick enough to coat the spoon. Stir in the cream, salt, pepper, nutmeg, and grated cheese, then pour the sauce over the cauliflower and bake in the oven for 20 minutes, or until golden brown on top.

Serve in the dish it was cooked in.

Baby Artichokes *à la Barigoule*
Artichauts "barigoule"

SERVES 4
PREPARATION TIME: 20 MINUTES
COOKING TIME: 45 MINUTES

8 baby artichokes, weighing about 1 ¼ lb. (600 g) in total

8 baby onions

4 medium mushrooms

4 large tomatoes

4 oz. (125 g) salt pork or bacon

3 tablespoons olive oil

2 cloves garlic

1 sprig thyme

¼ bay leaf

Salt and pepper

Bring 10 cups (2.5 liters) water to a boil in a large pot.

Cut off the leaves of each artichoke about a third of the way down from the top. Cut off the stems, then remove the tough outer leaves around the base and cut each artichoke into four pieces. Use a little spoon to scoop out the choke in the center of each piece. Quickly rinse the artichokes in warm water, then drop them into the boiling water, cook for 15 minutes, and drain.

Meanwhile, peel the onions. If small, leave them whole. Cut off any dirt on the stem of each mushroom, then wash the mushrooms and cut them into quarters. Blanch the tomatoes, peel them and chop them. Remove the rind from the bacon or salt pork. Dice the bacon or salt pork into ½-in. (1-cm) cubes and brown in an ungreased frying pan for 5 to 7 minutes.

Heat the oil in a high-sided frying pan or cast-iron pot. Add the tomatoes, mushrooms, onions, garlic, thyme, bay leaf, and salt pork or bacon. Cook for 10 to 20 minutes, or until half of the moisture from the vegetables has evaporated, then add the artichokes, salt, and pepper. Cover the pan and simmer for 25 minutes.

Serve immediately, either in the pan used to cook the artichokes or in a serving dish.

Note: Artichokes cooked this way are excellent cold as well as hot.

SERVES 4
PREPARATION TIME: 10 MINUTES
COOKING TIME: 15 MINUTES

1 lb. (500 g) morel mushrooms
Juice of 1 lemon
3 tablespoons (50 g) butter
½ cup (100 ml) cream
Salt and pepper

Morels in Cream
Morilles à la crème

Cut the morels into quarters if they are very large. Clean them and stew them in a pot with salt, pepper, lemon juice, and butter. Cook over fairly high heat with the lid on for about 10 minutes.

Pour almost all the cream into a small pan and reduce it a little. Pour the reduced cream into the morels and leave to simmer for a few minutes.

Just before serving, add the remaining cream to thicken the texture and make it whiter. Adjust the seasoning and serve.

Note: Morels are a popular garnish for fricassees with veal and poultry. They are also excellent in pies and dishes with puff pastry cases.

Imam Bayildi
Bayaldi

SERVES 5 TO 6
PREPARATION TIME: 15 MINUTES
COOKING TIME: 1 HOUR

2 small eggplants, weighing about 1 ¼ lb. (600 g) in total

5 medium (600 g) tomatoes

2 medium (250 g) onions

4 medium zucchini, weighing about 1 ½ lb. (700 g) in total

1 clove garlic

¼ bay leaf

1 sprig thyme

5 tablespoons (80 g) butter, plus butter for the dish

1 cup (100 g) grated Gruyère cheese

Salt and pepper

Preheat the oven to 350°F (180°C). Wash the vegetables and wipe them dry. Blanch and peel the tomatoes. Peel the onions. Cut the zucchini, eggplant, tomatoes, and onions into slices about ½ in. (1 cm) thick (if using a large eggplant rather than two smaller ones, cut it in half lengthwise before slicing). Keep all the vegetables separate from each other. Peel the garlic and crush it using the back of a fork. Crush the bay leaf.

Butter a large baking dish (preferably earthenware or enameled cast iron). Cover the bottom of the dish with the onions, then make a layer of zucchini and sprinkle with a little of the garlic, thyme, and bay leaf, salt, and pepper. Next, make a layer of eggplant, and lastly a layer of tomato, seasoning each layer as you did the zucchini. Dot the surface with half of the butter, then place in the oven for 30 minutes. At the end of this time, sprinkle with the cheese, dot with the remaining butter, and bake 20 to 30 minutes more or until golden brown on top. (If the vegetables dry out during the first 30 minutes' baking, cover them with foil; remove the foil for only the last 10 minutes of the baking time).

Variation: If preferred, the cheese can be omitted and ⅓ cup (80 ml) of olive oil used instead of butter. In this case, pour all of the oil over the surface of the vegetables before putting them in the oven. Instead of making layers as described here, you can simply make parallel lines of overlapping vegetables as shown in the photo, and bake them in individual baking dishes rather than in one large one.

The name of this Turkish dish means "the imam fainted," although there is disagreement as to whether the cause was its exquisite taste or the extravagant use of expensive olive oil.

4 ½ oz. (125 g) salt pork or bacon

2 ¼ lb. (1 kg) potatoes

1 lb. (500 g) tomatoes

3 tablespoons (50 g) butter, plus butter for the dish

1 sprig thyme

¼ bay leaf

About 1 cup (250 ml) water

Salt and pepper

Baked Potatoes with Tomatoes
Pommes boulangère

Preheat the oven to 425°F (210°C).

Remove the rind from the salt pork or bacon, and cut the salt pork or bacon into ½-in. (1-cm) cubes. Brown the salt pork or bacon in an ungreased frying pan, then drain on paper towels and reserve.

Peel the potatoes, wash them, and cut them into thin slices. Blanch the tomatoes, remove the hard part near the stem (peduncle), and slice the tomato. Reserve the juice from the tomato.

Lightly butter an earthenware or enameled cast-iron baking dish just large enough to hold the potatoes, then cover the bottom with a thin layer of potatoes, followed by a layer of tomatoes. Sprinkle over the bacon, thyme, bay leaf, salt, pepper, and a little butter. Cover this with a second layer of potatoes, and season them in the same way as the first. Fill the dish in this manner, layer after layer, then pour in the tomato juice and enough water to come about halfway up the potatoes. Place in the oven and bake 45 minutes to 1 hour, or until the potatoes are tender and the top layer has begun to brown. Serve in the baking dish.

Desserts

Vanilla Custard Sauce
Crème anglaise

SERVES 6
PREPARATION TIME: 30 MINUTES
COOKING TIME: 20 MINUTES

1 vanilla bean
2 cups (500 ml) milk
3 eggs
½ cup (3 ½ oz./100 g) granulated sugar
Salt

Split open the vanilla bean lengthwise, place in a medium saucepan (do not use an aluminum pan as this will blacken the sauce) with the milk and bring just to a boil. Remove the pan from the heat and leave to infuse for 7 to 8 minutes, then remove the vanilla bean.

Away from the heat, in the top of a double boiler, whisk together the eggs, sugar, and a pinch of salt, then whisk in the hot milk. Set the top of the double boiler in place and heat, stirring the mixture constantly for about 8 minutes or until it thickens (it should not boil). Immediately pour the sauce into a serving bowl and allow to cool, stirring occasionally before refrigerating.

Serve cold.

Serving suggestions: Serve with Chocolate Marble Cake (see p. 221). Vanilla custard sauce is also excellent with fresh fruit such as strawberries, raspberries, pears, etc.

Variation: Instead of vanilla, various other flavors can be given to the sauce: for example, stir a little chocolate, coffee, caramel, or rum into the sauce after it thickens but before it cools.

Pears in Red Wine
Poires au vin

SERVES 4
PREPARATION TIME: 10 MINUTES
COOKING TIME: 30 MINUTES

8 very small or 4 medium pears, weighing about 2 lb. (900 g) in total

Juice of ½ lemon

½ cup (100 g) granulated sugar

1 ¼ cups (300 ml) red wine

½ vanilla bean, split in half lengthwise

1 sprig thyme

2 peppercorns

1 clove

4 tablespoons (60 ml) *crème de cassis*

Preferably use a smooth-skinned variety of pear. Small ones need not be peeled (simply rinse them off and dry with a cloth); large ones can be peeled, cored, and then halved or quartered if desired (see Note).

Place the pears in a saucepan just large enough to hold them (stand small pears upright). Add the lemon juice, sugar, red wine, vanilla, thyme, peppercorns, clove, and *crème de cassis*. Bring just to a boil, then cover and simmer very slowly for 30 minutes.

Lift the pears out of the pan and stand them upright in a serving bowl. Pour the contents of the saucepan over them and leave to cool before serving (several hours will do, but overnight is best). Baste the pears periodically with the wine as they cool, and before serving.

Serving suggestions: Serve with Lyon-Style Fritters (see p. 189).

Note: Whole pears (even large ones) make for a nicer presentation. Peel them, then place them on their sides in the wine and turn over halfway through the cooking time. When done, stand them upright and baste as described for small pears.

Chocolate Mousse
Mousse au chocolat

SERVES 4 TO 5
PREPARATION TIME: 15 MINUTES
COOKING TIME: 10 MINUTES
RESTING TIME: AT LEAST 2 HOURS

4 ½ oz. (125 g)
bittersweet chocolate

2 tablespoons (30 g)
softened butter

4 tablespoons (50 g)
granulated sugar

4 eggs, separated

Chocolate mousse should be prepared at least 2 hours before serving; ideally, it should be made 24 hours ahead of time.

At least one hour ahead of time, take the butter and the eggs out of the refrigerator.

Break the chocolate into pieces.

Melt the chocolate and butter in a double boiler over low heat, stirring gently as they begin to melt. Stir in the sugar little by little. When thick and creamy, pour the chocolate mixture into a large mixing bowl and stir until it has cooled to lukewarm, then stir in the egg yolks.

Beat the egg whites until stiff in another mixing bowl, then slide them into the bowl with the chocolate and fold them in, using a wooden spatula or spoon.

When the egg whites have been completely incorporated into the chocolate, place the mousse in the refrigerator for 2 hours or more before serving.

Serving suggestions: Serve with warm almond cookies.

Yogurt Ice Cream
Glace au yaourt

SERVES 6
PREPARATION TIME: 15 MINUTES
CHILLING TIME: 30 MINUTES

8 egg yolks

⅔ cup (125 g) granulated sugar

2 cups (500 ml) plain yogurt

6 tablespoons (100 ml) crème fraîche or heavy cream

¼ cup (50 g) mixed candied fruit

Place the egg yolks in a bowl with the sugar and whisk until the mixture becomes smooth and pale in color. Stir in the yogurt, then the cream. Chop the candied fruit and add to the mixture. Pour into an ice cream maker and churn for 30 minutes or until stiff. You can serve the ice cream straightaway (it's best this way), or put it in containers and keep in a deep freezer for later use.

Serving suggestions: Serve with cookies, and a sauce made with fresh raspberries and a little sugar blended until smooth in a blender or food processor.

Rice Pudding
Riz au lait

SERVES 4
PREPARATION TIME: 10 MINUTES
COOKING TIME: 45 MINUTES

½ cup (100 g) round grain rice

1 vanilla bean

Generous 2 cups (500 ml) milk

½ cup (3 ½ oz./100 g) granulated sugar

½ teaspoon salt

Split the vanilla bean in half lengthwise. Place the milk, sugar, salt, and vanilla bean in a large saucepan and bring to a boil. Sprinkle in the rice, stirring.

Lower the heat (use a heat diffuser for very low, even heat) and cook the rice 45 minutes to 1 hour or until it is tender and has absorbed practically all of the milk (the milk left over will be absorbed as the rice cools).

Remove the vanilla bean, pour the rice into a bowl, and leave to cool; it can be served either warm or cold.

Serving suggestions: Serve with a homemade jam, poached fruits, or candied fruits.

Lyon-Style Fritters
Bugnes

SERVES 8
PREPARATION TIME: 15 MINUTES
COOKING TIME: 4 TO 6 MINUTES
RESTING TIME: AT LEAST 2 HOURS

1 ¾ sticks (200 g) butter

Zest of 1 lemon

5 cups (500 g) flour, sifted

1 pinch granulated sugar

1 teaspoon (5 g) baking powder

4 eggs

1 tablespoon (15 ml) rum

8 ½ cups (2 liters) peanut oil

Confectioners' sugar

Leave the butter at room temperature a little in advance, so that it is soft when you begin preparing the dough.

Grate the lemon zest very finely.

In a salad bowl, mix the flour, granulated sugar, and baking powder, then stir in the eggs one by one. Add the softened butter, the grated lemon zest, and the rum.

Work the mixture together with your fingertips until you obtain a malleable dough.

Heat the oil in a deep fryer or a large pan. Make sure that the temperature of the oil never gets too high (it should be simmering and not smoking; no higher than 350°F [180°C]).

On a floured working surface, spread out the dough in a very fine layer. Then, with the help of a scalloped pastry-wheel, cut the dough into more or less evenly shaped rectangles or triangles. Make a slit in the middle of each shape so that the dough swells up readily during cooking.

To check whether the oil has reached the right temperature, drop in a small piece of the dough, which should sizzle in the oil and quickly change color. When the oil is ready, carefully slide in the pieces of dough. As soon as the *bugnes* rise to the surface and turn a beautiful golden color, take them out and place them on paper towels.

Dust with confectioners' sugar before serving.

Jams and Jellies

Cooking times for jam vary depending on the ripeness of the fruit used. You can use a candy thermometer to test it: generally, when it reaches about 220°F (104°C) it is done. When cooked enough, most jams will bead, i.e., when dropped onto a clean plate, a drop will hold its shape and not collapse; when cool, it should stick to the plate if turned upside down.

FOR FIVE 1-LB. (450-G) JARS
PREPARATION TIME: 20 MINUTES
COOKING TIME: 40 MINUTES

5 lb. (2.25 kg) ripe fresh apricots

10 ½ cups (4 ½ lb. / 2 kg) granulated sugar

2 cups (500 ml) water

Apricot Jam
Confiture d'abricots

Wash the fruit in cold water, drain, and pat dry in a towel. Cut open each apricot and remove the pit; you need 4 quarts (2 kg) of apricot halves for making the jam. Place half of the apricots in a preserving pan, add the sugar and water, and bring to a boil, stirring frequently. Once the water boils, add the remaining apricots and boil for 20 minutes or until the jam is bubbling thickly and coats a spoon. The jam has cooked enough when it beads (see note above). When the jam is done, remove it from the heat and ladle into clean jars. Allow to cool completely, before covering the jars with cellophane for storing.

FOR ABOUT SEVEN TO EIGHT
1-LB. (450-G) JARS
PREPARATION TIME: 15 MINUTES
COOKING TIME: 50 MINUTES

4 ½ lb. (2 kg) fresh ripe raspberries

10 ½ cups (4 ½ lb. / 2 kg) granulated sugar

2 cups (500 ml) water

Raspberry Jam
Confiture de framboises

Wash and quickly drain the raspberries. Remove any remaining stems. Place the raspberries in a preserving pan with the sugar and water and bring to a boil, stirring gently. Boil for 30 minutes or until the jam coats a spoon and beads (see note above). When done, remove the jam from the heat and ladle into clean jars. Allow to cool completely before covering the jars with cellophane for storing.

Quince Jellies
Pâte de coings

SERVES 10
PREPARATION TIME: 15 MINUTES
COOKING TIME:
1 HOUR 20 MINUTES

---

2 ¼ lb. (1 kg) quinces
About 1 ½ lb. (700 g) granulated
sugar, plus sugar
to sprinkle over and to serve

Use only perfectly ripe, unbruised quinces. Peel them and cut the pulp off of the hard, central core. Cut the quinces into quarters. Place in a preserving pan with just enough water to barely cover, bring to a boil and boil rapidly for about 20 minutes or until the quinces are very soft and the water has evaporated.

Purée the quinces in a food mill, using a fine grill, or in a blender or food processor. Weigh or measure the purée and place it back in the preserving pan. Add the same weight of sugar to the purée, or for every cup (250 g) of purée, add 1 ¼ cups (250 g) of granulated sugar. Bring to a boil and boil for 40 minutes, or until the jelly is extremely thick, stirring almost constantly; if the jelly splatters while cooking, lower the heat.

Pour the jelly into a shallow porcelain pie dish or earthenware platter–it should be no more than 1 in. (2.5 cm) thick.

Preheat the oven to 250°F (120°C).

Sprinkle the surface of the jelly with a little sugar, then place in the oven for 20 minutes to dry out. Remove from the oven and allow to cool completely, then cut the jelly into long bands. Wrap each band in parchment paper or waxed paper and store in a cool, dry place (do not refrigerate), or serve immediately.

To serve, cut the bands into squares, roll them in granulated sugar, and arrange on a plate or platter.

MAKES ABOUT 4 CUPS (1 L)
PREPARATION TIME: 10 MINUTES
COOKING TIME: 15 MINUTES

Creamy Chocolate Sauce
Sauce crème au chocolat

9 oz. (250 g) bittersweet chocolate,

or

1 generous cup (4 ½ oz./125 g) unsweetened cocoa powder and ⅓ cup (75 ml) water and ⅔ cup (4 ½ oz./125 g) sugar

¾ cup (200 ml) crème fraîche or heavy cream

2 tablespoons (30 g) butter

Melt the chocolate in a double-boiler, or heat the cocoa powder with the water and sugar, stirring from time to time.

When the chocolate is melted, or the cocoa comes to a boil, remove from the heat, and add the cream and butter. Whisk briskly for 2 minutes.

Madeleines

MAKES 24 LARGE MADELEINES
PREPARATION TIME: 15 MINUTES
COOKING TIME: 20 MINUTES

1 ¼ sticks (150 g) butter

Generous ⅔ cup (150 g) granulated sugar

1 tablespoon orange flower water

3 eggs

1 ½ cups (150 g) flour

At least one hour ahead of time, take the eggs and butter out of the refrigerator.

Preheat the oven to 425°F (210°C).

Melt the butter in a small saucepan. Place the sugar, orange flower water, and eggs in a mixing bowl and beat with a whisk. Whisk in the melted butter, then add the flour little by little, whisking constantly to make a smooth batter.

Lightly butter the madeleine molds, then fill them to about three-quarters with the batter. Bake for 20 minutes, until a rich golden brown, then turn out onto a cake rack and allow to cool before serving.

Variation: Orange flower water can be replaced by a tablespoon of finely grated orange peel or lemon peel if preferred.

Note: Madeleines are usually baked in elongated, shell-shaped molds, but any shallow cupcake or cookie mold could be used for baking them.

SERVES 4
PREPARATION TIME: 20 MINUTES
COOKING TIME: 20 MINUTES

2 ½ tablespoons (40 g) softened butter, plus butter for the molds

Scant ½ cup (90 g) granulated sugar, plus sugar for the molds

1 ⅓ cup (300 ml) milk

3 tablespoons flour

6 egg yolks

9 egg whites

Confectioners' sugar (to sprinkle on top)

Plain Soufflé
Soufflé bonne femme

Preheat the oven to 425°F (210°C).

Lightly butter four individual soufflé molds about 4 in. (10 cm) wide. Sprinkle in some sugar and turn to coat the sides of the molds with it. Pour out any excess sugar, then place the molds upside down on a large platter in the refrigerator while making the soufflé batter.

Place ¾ cup (200 ml) of milk in a saucepan with the sugar and bring to a boil. Meanwhile, stir the remaining 6 tablespoons (100 ml) of milk into the flour. Pour the flour mixture into the boiling milk, stirring, then simmer very slowly for 3 minutes, stirring occasionally. Allow to cool for 2 minutes, then place in a mixing bowl and stir in the butter and the egg yolks. Beat the egg whites until stiff, then fold them into the other ingredients. Pour the soufflé batter into the molds and bake for about 20 minutes. Sprinkle with a little confectioners' sugar as soon as they come from the oven, and serve immediately.

Variation: When adding the egg yolks, you can add 2 tablespoons (or more to taste) of rum, cognac, Grand Marnier, or any other alcohol to the batter to flavor it.

Note: *This soufflé batter can be made and poured into the molds up to half an hour before baking.*

Dried Apricot Soufflé
Soufflé aux abricots

SERVES 4
PREPARATION TIME: 20 MINUTES
COOKING TIME: 30 MINUTES

2 tablespoons (30g) softened butter (for the molds)

2 tablespoons granulated sugar, plus sugar for the molds

4 ½ oz. (125 g) dried apricots (see Note)

2 tablespoons water

2 egg yolks

4 egg whites

Preheat the oven to 425°F (210°C).

Butter four individual soufflé molds about 4 in. (10 cm) wide. Sprinkle sugar into each one and turn to coat the sides with it. Pour out any excess sugar, then place the molds upside down on a plate in the refrigerator while making the soufflé batter.

Chop the apricots to a fine paste. Place the water and sugar in a small saucepan and bring just to a boil. Remove from the heat and stir in first the apricots, then the egg yolks; pour into a large mixing bowl and reserve.

Whisk the egg whites until stiff, then fold them into the apricot mixture. Pour the soufflé batter into the molds and bake for about 25 minutes or until golden brown on top (don't open the oven door, but check by looking through the window in it, to avoid causing a drop in temperature that could make the soufflé sink). Serve immediately.

Serve with blackcurrant jelly and cookies.

Note: Be sure to use very soft apricots when making this dish.

SERVES 6
PREPARATION TIME: 10 MINUTES
RESTING TIME: 1 HOUR
COOKING TIME:
5 MINUTES PER CRÊPE

3 tablespoons (50 g) butter, plus
butter (or oil) for the pan
2 ½ cups (9 oz./250 g) flour
1 tablespoon granulated sugar
3 eggs
2 cups (500 ml) milk
Salt

Crêpes
Pâte à crêpe

At least one hour ahead of time, take the eggs, butter, and milk out of the refrigerator.

Melt the butter in a small saucepan and reserve.

Place the flour, sugar, and salt in a mixing bowl; stir in the eggs, then pour in the milk little by little, stirring at first, then whisking to make a smooth, liquid batter. Finally whisk in the melted butter. Leave the batter at room temperature for about 1 hour before making the crêpes.

Lightly butter or oil a frying pan (preferably cast-iron or nonstick). When very hot, spoon about ¼ cup (60 ml) of the batter into the center of it, and tip and turn the frying pan to cover the bottom with the batter and make a very thin pancake (crêpe). Cook the crêpe for about 2 minutes over moderate heat, turn it over using a flexible-blade spatula, and finish cooking about 3 minutes on the second side. Remove the crêpe and lightly butter the pan before cooking the next one. To keep the crêpes warm after cooking, heat a little water to simmering in a saucepan. Set a large plate on top of the saucepan. As the crêpes finish cooking, put them on the plate and cover with a second plate turned upside down.

Serve the crêpes hot with honey, walnuts, jam, or chestnut cream. They are also delicious simply spread with a little butter and sprinkled with granulated sugar.

6 eggs, or
4 eggs plus 3 egg yolks

½ teaspoon sugar

2 tablespoons crème fraîche
or heavy cream

Salt

Butter for cooking

Confectioners' sugar for dusting

Special equipment:
a metal skewer

Sweet Omelet
Omelet au sucre

Whip the crème fraîche and set aside. Beat the eggs, but not too much, with a pinch of salt. Add the sugar and fold in the whipped cream.

Cook the omelet in butter, turn it onto a warmed dish, and dust it with confectioners' sugar.

Heat a skewer until it is almost red hot. Use it to draw out a criss-cross pattern that will turn a nice caramel color.

Serve immediately.

Lemon Tart
Tarte au citron

SERVES 6 TO 8
PREPARATION TIME: 20 MINUTES
RESTING TIME: 1 HOUR
COOKING TIME: 45 MINUTES
CHILLING TIME: 3 HOURS

DOUGH

2 ½ cups (250 g) flour

1 stick (125 g) softened butter

6 tablespoons (75 g)
granulated sugar

1 egg

FILLING

Juice of 3 lemons

Zest of 3 lemons

7 tablespoons (100 g)
softened butter

⅔ cup (125 g) granulated sugar

3 eggs

2 tablespoons (30 ml) crème
fraîche or heavy cream

About one hour and a half ahead of time, take the butter out of the refrigerator. Break the butter into pieces.

First make the dough: place the flour, butter, sugar, and egg in a large mixing bowl. Use your fingers to "pinch" the ingredients together, working quickly, until a ball of dough is formed. Place it on a lightly floured table or plate, cover with a clean towel, and leave for 1 hour before baking.

Preheat the oven to 350°F (180°C). Lightly butter and flour a 9 ½-in. (24-cm) pie pan, then roll the dough out into a thin sheet and line the pan. Cut off any excess dough from around the edges, then prick the bottom in several places with the prongs of a fork. Place a piece of parchment paper on top of the dough; it should be large enough to cover the bottom and sides of the dough and stick up above the edges of the pan. Press the paper well against the dough lining the sides of the pan, then fill the pan with uncooked rice, beans, or lentils. Place in the oven and bake for 15 minutes, then remove from the oven and lower the oven temperature to 250°F (120°C). Carefully lift out the paper containing the rice or beans (save the rice or beans for baking other pie crusts in the same way).

Wash the lemons and carefully dry them. Thinly grate the zest and set aside. Squeeze the juice from the lemons and set aside.

Make the filling by beating together first the butter and sugar, beat in the eggs and cream, then add the lemon juice and zest. Pour the filling into the pie crust, place back in the oven and bake for about 30 minutes or until the filling and crust have begun to brown. Allow to cool completely, then chill in the refrigerator for 3 hours before serving.

SERVES 4
PREPARATION TIME: 5 MINUTES
COOKING TIME:
ABOUT 10 MINUTES

French Eggnog
Lait de poule

4 egg yolks

4 tablespoons (50 g) granulated sugar

4 mugs milk

At least one hour ahead of time, take the eggs and the milk out of the refrigerator.

Place the egg yolks and sugar in a mixing bowl and whisk lightly to combine. Bring the milk to a boil in a saucepan, then remove from the heat and wait for 5 minutes before adding it to the egg yolks. Whisk in the hot milk little by little, then pour into the mugs or bowls and serve immediately.

Variation: You can flavor the eggnog, if you like, with a little rum or cognac to taste just before serving; for children, flavor it with a little coffee, chocolate, or orange flower water.

In France, lait de poule *("hen's milk," if literally translated) is said to be very good for you if you have a bad cold or the flu.*

SERVES 4
PREPARATION TIME: 5 MINUTES
COOKING TIME: ABOUT 8 MINUTES

Hot Spiced Wine
Vin chaud

3 ¼ cups (750 ml) good red wine

10 lumps light brown sugar

1 large pinch cinnamon

1 clove

1 lemon

Place the wine, sugar, cinnamon, and clove in a saucepan and bring to a boil.

While the wine is heating up, wash the lemon, dry in a towel, and cut four thin slices from it. Place one slice of lemon in each glass. Squeeze the remaining lemon and add the juice to the pan with the wine. As soon as the wine boils, remove the clove, then pour the wine into the glasses and serve.

Hot spiced wine is excellent for you when you feel a cold coming on.

SERVES 6
PREPARATION TIME: 30 MINUTES
COOKING TIME: 40 MINUTES

2 ¼ lb. (1 kg) apples, preferably Reinette du Canada, or other russet variety

3 tablespoons (50 g) sugar

3 tablespoons (50 g) butter

1 vanilla bean

Zest of ½ lemon

2 tablespoons dry white wine

1 sandwich loaf

4 tablespoons Apricot Jam (see p. 191)

Melted butter for the slices of bread

Apple Charlotte
Charlotte reine du Canada

Generously butter the charlotte mold. Peel the apples, quarter them, and remove the seeds and cores. Place the quarters in a saucepan and sprinkle with the sugar. Cut the butter into cubes and dot them among the apple. Slit the vanilla bean lengthways. Add the lemon zest and vanilla bean to the apple mixture and pour in the white wine. Cook gently, stirring from time to time, and then turn up the heat to reduce until very thick. While the apples are cooking, melt the apricot jam and push through a sieve. Mix it into the applesauce and leave to cool.

Preheat the oven to 500°F (260°C), or as high as it will go. Cut slices of bread ⅛ in. (4 mm) thick–just enough to make 12 right-angled triangles. Dip them in the melted butter. Line the bottom of the charlotte mold with them, butter side down, packing them closely together so that the apple mixture does not seep through.

Then cut ¼-in. (1-cm) thick slices and cut them into rectangles measuring 1 ¼ in. (4 cm) wide and just under 1 in. (2 cm) longer than the side of the mold (unless your mold is very high, in which case they should be the same length). Dip each rectangle in melted butter and place them, butter side towards the side of the mold, overlapping one another until you have lined the sides.

Remove the vanilla bean and lemon zest from the apple mixture and fill the charlotte mold. Cut a piece of bread into a circle ⅛ in. (4 mm) thick (or use enough bread to make a circle), dip it in melted butter, and enclose the apple mixture with it. Immediately place in the very hot oven so that the bread browns instead of going soggy, and cook for about 40 minutes. Leave to rest for 15 minutes before turning it out of the mold. Unmold it only when you are ready to serve.

My Grandmother's Waffles
Gaufres de grand-mère Bocuse

MAKES 20 WAFFLES
PREPARATION TIME: 20 MINUTES
COOKING TIME: 15 MINUTES

5 cups (1 lb./500 g) flour
1 pinch baking powder
1 tablespoon sugar
1 cup (250 ml) milk
3 cup (750 ml) whipping cream (30 percent butterfat)
8 egg yolks
⅓ cup (75 ml) rum
1 ¼ cups (300 g) melted butter
4 egg whites
Salt
Butter to grease the waffle iron

In a mixing bowl, combine the flour, baking powder, sugar, and a pinch of salt.

Pour in first the milk, then the cream, the egg yolks, and the rum, stirring thoroughly each time. Then incorporate the melted butter. Whip the egg whites until they form firm peaks and fold them into the batter.

Heat the waffle iron and butter the plates. Pour some batter onto one of its sides, making sure the dimples are filled. Close the waffle iron and turn it over so that the batter is distributed on both plates.

This will ensure that your waffles are nice and crisp.

Serving suggestions: Serve your waffles simply dusted with confectioners' sugar, topped with Chantilly cream or spread with homemade preserves.

PREPARATION TIME: 30 MINUTES
COOKING TIME: 15 MINUTES

2 lb. 3 oz. (1 kg) ripe raspberries
About 5 ¼ cups (1 kg) sugar

Raspberry Syrup
Sirop de framboises au naturel

Wash the raspberries and press them through a fine sieve. Place them into a pan, bring to a boil, and simmer for a few minutes. Strain the fruit pulp, weigh it, then add an equal quantity (by weight) of sugar. Return the raspberry pulp and sugar to the pan and heat gently until the sugar has dissolved.

PREPARATION TIME: 40 MINUTES
COOKING TIME: 45 MINUTES

About 1 lb. 5 oz. (600 g) *marron*-quality chestnuts (unseparated; one piece per nut)
1 vanilla bean

SYRUP
4 cups (1 l) water
1 lb. 2 oz. (500 g sugar)

Special equipment:
a Baumé scale (hydrometer or saccharometer), to measure the sugar density of the syrup

Candied Chestnuts
Marrons confits

Peel the chestnuts without breaking them. Place them in a saucepan and simmer gently in a *blanc* (water to which a small amount of flour has been added) for about 10 minutes. Drain, then place them in a glass or earthenware jar with the vanilla pod.

To prepare the syrup, pour the water into a perfectly clean copper pot and bring to a simmer. Add the sugar and heat until a syrup is obtained. When the syrup reaches 20°Bé (measure the sugar density using the Baumé scale), pour the boiling syrup over the chestnuts. Set the chestnuts aside for 48 hours, as well as the remaining syrup.

48 hours later, reheat the syrup until it reaches 24°Bé (use the Baumé scale to check the sugar density) and pour it over the chestnuts. Repeat this process twice more, reheating the syrup until it reaches a density of 28°Bé and 32°Bé respectively, at 48-hour intervals.

For the final glazing, reheat the syrup until it reaches a density of 36°Bé. Remove from the heat. Using a spatula, immerse the chestnuts in the syrup and mix until the chestnuts are completely coated. Remove and place on a drying rack or tray to set.

SERVES 4
PREPARATION TIME: 40 MINUTES
CHILLING TIME: 3 HOURS

2 cups (500 ml) puréed cherries

Cherries for garnish

2 tablespoons maraschino liqueur, plus a little extra to poach the cherries

16 egg yolks

2 ⅔ cups (1 lb./500 g) sugar

2 cups (500 ml) milk

2 cups (500 ml) crème fraîche or heavy cream

⅔ oz. (20 g) gum tragacanth, finely crushed (available from specialty cake decorating stores or online; see Note)

Raspberry coulis

Iced Cherry Soufflé
Soufflé glacé aux cerises

Remove the stems and pits from the cherries you will be using for garnish. Poach them in a syrup flavored with maraschino liqueur. Leave them to cool completely.

Beat the egg yolks and sugar together until the mixture is pale and thick. Pour just a little milk over the mixture, whisk it, and then return it all to the saucepan. Return to moderate heat, stirring all the time, until the mixture thickens and coats the back of the spoon. Remove from the heat and stir frequently until cooled.

Then stir in the crème fraîche, finely crushed gum tragacanth, and puréed cherries.

Place the mixing bowl over ice and whisk vigorously until very frothy and slightly thickened.

Line the sides of four soufflé molds with parchment paper; it should be 2 in. (5 cm) higher than the rim.

Fill the soufflé molds to just under ½ in. (1 cm) from the top of the strip of parchment paper. Smooth the surface with an offset spatula. Top with the poached cherries and chill for 3 hours in the refrigerator.

Just before serving, remove the strip of parchment paper and drizzle lightly with very cold raspberry coulis.

Note: Gum tragacanth is the dried sap or gum obtained from a Middle-Eastern plant, often used in gum paste for cake decoration. An alternative that is slightly more widely available (but synthetic) is tylose powder.

SERVES 4
PREPARATION TIME: 20 MINUTES

Fruit Salad
Salade de fruits

2 apples

2 pears (not too ripe)

1 orange

½ grapefruit

½ pineapple

Juice of 1 lemon

1 cup (100 g) walnut meats

¼ cup (50 g) granulated sugar

2 bananas

6 mint leaves

Peel and core the apples and pears, and cut them into quarters. Place the apples and pears in a large salad bowl.

Use a knife to cut off the peel (including the white inner skin) of the orange and grapefruit, then cut out the wedges and add them to the bowl, along with any juice they gave out.

Cut the skin off of the pineapple, cut out the central core, then cut it into wedges and add to the salad. Add the lemon juice, walnut meats, and sugar. Stir gently, then refrigerate for about 1 hour before serving.

Just before serving, peel and slice the bananas and add them, finely chop the mint and sprinkle over the fruit, and serve.

Serving suggestions: Serve with almond cookies.

Variation: All kinds of fruits other than the ones used here can be used in fruit salads; for example tropical fruits such as kiwis or lychees, or fresh grapes are all excellent additions to a fruit salad. If you like, 3 tablespoons (50 ml) of brandy or a fruit brandy can be added to the salad at the same time as the lemon juice.

SERVES 4
PREPARATION TIME: 10 MINUTES
COOKING TIME: 20 MINUTES

2 ¼ lb. (1 kg) apples

4 tablespoons (60 ml) water

¼ cup (50 g) granulated sugar

Either 1 pinch cinnamon or
lemon juice to taste,
or
½ cup (70 g) light brown sugar
and 2 tablespoons water

Applesauce
Compote de pommes

Peel, quarter, and seed the apples, then cut into thin slices. Place in a saucepan with the water and sugar, and simmer uncovered for 20 minutes, stirring occasionally with a wooden spoon.

You can either flavor the applesauce with cinnamon or lemon juice, or with caramel. In the second case, make a caramel by cooking the brown sugar and water together until the mixture darkens and caramelizes. Stir the hot applesauce into the caramel and serve warm.

Cherry Clafoutis
Clafoutis

SERVES 6
PREPARATION TIME: 20 MINUTES
COOKING TIME: ABOUT 1 HOUR

1 lb. (500 g) dark, ripe cherries

1 ½ teaspoons (5 g) baking powder

2 cups (200 g) flour

3 eggs

¼ cup (50 g) granulated sugar, plus sugar to finish

2 cups (500 ml) milk

Salt

2 tablespoons (30 g) butter (for the pan)

Preheat the oven to 350°F (180°C).

Wash the cherries, dry them in a clean cloth and remove the stems, but do not pit them. Reserve.

Mix the baking powder and flour together in a mixing bowl, then push it up against the sides of the bowl to form a well in the center. Break the eggs into the well, add the sugar, milk, and a pinch of salt, and stir, mixing the flour in as it falls from the sides. The finished batter should be smooth; if there are any lumps, work the batter through a sieve to eliminate them.

Butter a 10-in. (25-cm) pie or cake pan (preferably porcelain). Stir the cherries into the batter, then pour it into the pan and bake for 45 minutes to 1 hour. When golden brown, remove the clafoutis from the oven and sprinkle with sugar. Serve either hot or cold in the pan.

SERVES 6
PREPARATION TIME: 20 MINUTES
COOKING TIME: 45 MINUTES

1 stick (120 g) softened butter, plus butter for the mold

2 large eggs

⅔ cup (120 g) granulated sugar

1 ¼ cups (125 g) flour

1 ¾ oz. (50 g) bittersweet chocolate

Salt

Chocolate Marble Cake
Marbré au chocolat

One hour and a half ahead of time, take the eggs and the butter out of the refrigerator.

Preheat the oven to 350°F (180°C). Place the butter in a bowl near a source of heat to soften, but don't let it melt.

Break the eggs into a teacup to check they are fresh. Beat the eggs and sugar in a mixing bowl until smooth and a pale yellow color, then sift in the flour, whisking as it is being added. Whisk in the softened butter and a pinch of salt; the finished batter should be smooth.

Melt the chocolate in a double boiler.

Lightly butter a 9 ½-in. (24-cm) pound cake or loaf pan, line it with parchment paper, then lightly butter the paper as well. Pour the melted chocolate over the batter, then barely stir it in, so that there will be light and dark patches. Pour the batter into the mold, smooth the surface, and bake for 45 minutes. Test to see if the cake is done by sticking a needle or knife blade into the center; it should come out clean and dry. If not, bake the cake a little longer.

Turn the mold upside down on a cake rack to cool as soon as you take the cake from the oven, but don't lift it off the cake until it has cooled completely. When cool, lift off the mold, peel off the paper, turn right side up and serve on a serving platter.

This cake will stay fresh for up to a week, wrapped in aluminum foil.

Serving suggestions: Serve with Vanilla Custard Sauce (see p. 184) or Chocolate Mousse (see p. 186) on the side.

SERVES 8
PREPARATION TIME: 30 MINUTES
CHILLING TIME: 30 MINUTES
COOKING TIME: 20 MINUTES

SWEETENED SHORT PASTRY
(CRUMBLED)
(Makes about 9 oz./250 g pastry)

1 cup (4 ¼ oz./125 g) flour

½ teaspoon (2 g) salt

1 heaped tablespoon (15 g)
sugar

6 ½ tablespoons (95 g) butter,
softened

1 egg

A few spoonfuls milk (or cream,
or water)

FILLING

1 lb. (500 g) strawberries

3 oz. (80 g) redcurrant jelly (jam)

2 tablespoons kirsch

A few pistachios, chopped

Strawberry Tart
Tarte aux fraises

Sweetened Short Pastry

Sift the flour onto the work surface and shape it into a circle with a well in the center. In the well, place the salt, sugar, softened butter, egg, and milk (or cream or water).

Using your fingers, dissolve the salt in the liquid in the center, gradually combine the butter with the liquid, and work the flour into the center of the well to mix it with the other ingredients. If necessary, sprinkle a little water over with your fingertips. The dough must not be too firm. Do not overwork it, otherwise it will be tough. Chill for about 30 minutes.

Roll out the pastry and fit it into an 8-in. (20-cm) tart circle if you have one. Otherwise use a tart pan with a detachable bottom. Push the pastry in gently, making sure it fits the inside of the circle snugly.

Bake the pastry case blind at 350°F (180°C).

When it is done (it should be nicely browned), leave it to cool. Remove the circle or detach it from the pan when it is almost cool.

Shortly before serving, brush the pastry crust with half the redcurrant jelly. Arrange the strawberries attractively over it.

Dilute the remaining jelly with the kirsch and glaze the surface with it. Sprinkle with the chopped pistachios.

Appendixes

Useful Information and General Advice

BUTTER

Use only unsalted butter in these recipes. Butter should always be of the highest quality, and no substitutes (such as margarine) should be used if you want an authentic version of these dishes.

Butter is often said to be "softened." This means that it has been left at room temperature for about an hour or until it can easily be broken into soft pieces with your fingers. It is extremely important that butter be sufficiently soft whenever sauces or doughs are being made. *See* Softening or Creaming Butter.

CARAMELIZING (COOKING SUGAR)

Recipes will call for sugar to be caramelized to various stages or colors, depending on the strength of flavor required. The darker the color, the stronger the flavor. There are two methods for caramelizing sugar: the dry method, when the sugar is cooked directly in the pan, and the wet method, using water. To make a dry caramel, pour the sugar out into an even layer in a heavy bottomed pan or skillet over medium heat and cook until it liquefies and reaches the desired color. The second method is easier to control. Dissolve the specified quantity of sugar in water, bring to a boil, and reduce until the sugar is caramelized. With both methods, great caution should be exercised so that you don't burn yourself, and it should be watched carefully so that it does not burn (sugar burns extremely quickly).

To line a baking pan with a caramel, pour it into the pan as soon as it is ready and swirl it around as quickly as possible until the pan is evenly coated. It will set almost as soon as it comes into contact with the cold surface.

EGGS

Unless otherwise specified, always use 1-oz. (50-g) eggs, or 21 oz. (596 g) per dozen. These are labeled "medium" on the package. If using much smaller or much larger eggs, adjust the number used, as appropriate.

In the chapter on eggs in this book, you can use any size of egg you wish.

FLOUR

All-purpose flour can be used throughout the book. Do not sift the flour when measuring or when using unless expressly advised to do so.

FOLDING

Stiffly beaten egg whites (and whipped cream) are folded into other ingredients rather than stirred, to keep them from collapsing. To fold, spoon about a third of the beaten egg whites on to the ingredients they are to be mixed with. Using a flat, wooden spatula (a wooden spoon may be used, but it's not as efficient), cut down through the egg whites to the bottom of the bowl, then lift or scoop the other ingredients up onto the egg whites, giving the bowl a quarter-turn as you do so. Repeat this motion until the two are mixed together, then add the remaining egg whites and continue in the same manner. The final mixture should be perfectly homogenous, with no unmixed particles in it.

GELATIN SHEETS

Gelatin in thin transparent sheets (or leaves) weighing precisely 2 grams is the form used in France. They are available from specialty stores or online. To use them, soak them in a bowl of very cold water (unless otherwise specified) for about 10 to 15 minutes, until they are softened and very pliable. Then remove them from the water and squeeze all the liquid out with your hands. Dissolve them in the quantity of warm liquid specified in your recipe, stirring until there are no visible traces left. Follow the recipe instructions for setting or jelling times. Note that gelatin is an animal-derived product; should you prefer a plant-based jelling agent (such as agar-agar), follow the instructions on the packet for quantities and times.

GROUND ALMONDS (ALMOND MEAL)

Sweet, blanched, ground almonds are a staple of French pastry making. To make your own, place blanched almonds (peel removed) in a food processor and pulse until they are reduced to a fine powder–essential for best baking results.

HERBS

Various fresh herbs, such as tarragon, chervil, and parsley are frequently called for in these recipes. Whenever possible, try to use the herb in question; otherwise, substitute more available fresh herbs rather than using dried ones. For instance, fresh chives or parsley, or a little mint or basil, could be used in many recipes that call for chervil.

MIXING BOWLS

There are two main types of mixing bowl: flat-bottomed, which can be used for most purposes, and round-bottomed, which allows a whisk to reach the lower levels of a liquid, making it ideal for whisking egg whites and cream or preparing mayonnaise.

OILS

There are basically two kinds of oil: those that withstand high heat (and thus can be used for frying) and those that cannot. The first type is generally referred to as cooking oil, the second as salad or seasoning oil. Choose your oils carefully. Neutral oils are preferable for cooking, as well as for some salads; peanut oil and sunflower oil can be used for both, as can corn oil.

Specific oils, especially olive oil, are sometimes called for. Use only the best, cold-pressed olive oil–the results are appreciably better than with less expensive oils.

PEELING

Most vegetables can simply be peeled with a vegetable peeler or knife, but certain fruits and vegetables are peeled using hot water to remove the outer skin. Tomatoes are peeled by dipping them very briefly (10 seconds or so) in boiling water. This causes the skin to pull away from the flesh. Drain and cool immediately under cold running water. To peel almonds, leave them for about one minute in boiling water, transfer them to cold water until they are cool enough to handle, and slide the skin off.

Most vegetables, including tomatoes, can be peeled and chopped up to an hour or two before being used in a recipe, but potatoes should be peeled right before being cooked, because they tend to discolor when exposed to air. Peeled potatoes should not be left in a basin of water–they will lose their taste and vitamins.

PREHEATING
An oven must be preheated before placing food in it to roast or bake. Allow 15 to 20 minutes for the oven to heat to the correct temperature. This will ensure that the cooking times given are accurate and the food properly cooked.

SAUCES (CLASSIC FRENCH)
Marie-Antoine (Antonin) Carême (1783-1833) is considered one of the founders of classic French cuisine. The author of a number of authoritative books, he classified its sauces, dividing the hot sauces into white and brown sauces. White sauces begin with a roux (see glossary, Thickening or Enriching); the béchamel takes milk while the velouté uses a white stock, whether poultry, veal, or fish. All other white sauces are derived from one of these two. A Mornay sauce is a béchamel to which cheese is added, and Aurore sauce is either a béchamel or velouté with a tomato flavoring. The three basic brown sauces that give rise to innumerable derivatives are the espagnole, tomato, and *demi-glace*. Sauces often bear the names of their place of origin: Périgueux sauce adds truffles to the *demi-glace*; bordelaise sauce is made with Bordeaux wine.

There are four basic methods for sauce making: simple mixing together, as in a vinaigrette; emulsifying, often with eggs, such as mayonnaise and its derivatives (tartare sauce, for example); adding stock or other liquid to a roux; and reducing and thickening a stock.

SOFTENING OR CREAMING BUTTER
Many recipes require butter to be softened: bring it to room temperature and pound it or work it with a wooden spoon or spatula. At this stage, it is known in French as *beurre pommade*, creamed butter. For best baking results, butter should be at room temperature.

STOCK
An essential ingredient in the French kitchen, stock may be white or brown. White stock is made with white meat (or poultry) and bones that are boiled with aromatic ingredients and then filtered. To make brown stock, roast the bones and aromatic ingredients until they brown and then boil in water before filtering. Stocks should not be salted, as they are used to make sauces that have to be seasoned.

THERMOMETERS
A thermometer is a useful kitchen tool to check that food has reached the correct temperature. They are used mostly for meat (meat or instant-read thermometer) to ensure that it is properly cooked, to check on its progress in the oven, or to avoid overcooking; for sugar (candy thermometer) to measure the temperature of a sugar solution and identify the stage of cooking reached; and for fat, which is helpful for deep frying. Candy and fat thermometers are able to read very high temperatures (up to 400°F/200°C).

WARMING (SERVING DISHES AND FOOD)
Any hot food should preferably be served on hot plates or serving platters. To warm them, simply place them in a moderately hot oven for 5 to 10 minutes, leaving the oven door ajar so they don't heat too much. If the oven is being used, you can

either place the plates or platters in the drawer under the oven to warm for at least 20 minutes, or set them over a large pot of boiling water and cover them with a large lid or another plate turned upside down. All these methods can be used for keeping foods warm as well; this is generally required when sauces using the pan juices are made at the last minute.

WEIGHING AND MEASURING

For precision, French chefs–pastry chefs in particular–weigh all of their ingredients, and scales are a basic tool in many French home kitchens. Measurements are given here in both the American (imperial) and French (metric) systems. The metric system is easier and more exact, but since few home cooks have scales in the US, quantities are given, wherever possible, in cup and spoon measurements. It is necessary to bear in mind, however, that the conversion of quantities inevitably results in some rounding down or up. For the more straightforward recipes, these small differences will have little impact on the end result. However, we recommend weighing your ingredients wherever possible, and advise against mixing imperial and metric measurements in the same recipe.

Some general rules on measuring might be appropriate here:
– Never sift flour into the measuring cup unless expressly advised to do so; measure it directly from the package or canister. If it must be sifted, sift after measuring.
– Never pack ingredients into a cup unless advised to do so.
– Teaspoon and tablespoon measurements should *always* be level, unless accompanied by the word "scant" or "generous." "Scant" means that the spoon is almost full, but not quite. "Generous" means that the ingredient forms a gentle mound above the edge of the spoon rather than being level with it.

– When applied to cup measurements, "scant" means that the ingredient comes almost up to the line indicating the measurement, but not quite–it should never be more than 1 fluid ounce (½ cup) below the line. "Generous" means that the ingredient should rise slightly above the line indicating the measurement, but never more than 1 fluid ounce (½ cup) above it.

For convenience, solid butter measurements are given in one of two forms: either tablespoons, for small quantities, or sticks, for large quantities. Since not all butter is packaged in sticks, you may find the following information useful: 1 stick = 4 oz. = 8 tablespoons.

WHISKING

Whenever the term "whisk" is used, it means to beat with a wire (hand) whisk, never with an electric mixer. It is employed especially in connection with sauces, many of which require the use of a wire whisk if they are to be made successfully.

Two main types of whisk exist: balloon whisks, which are short and rounded, and are used for whisking egg whites, and sauce whisks, which have stiffer wires and are longer.

WINE

Sometimes specific red or white wines are suggested for cooking. These suggestions are always optional, but if they are followed, the wine in question should be French (i.e., a French Burgundy rather than a Californian one). Otherwise, when cooking, use only a wine that you would consider good enough to drink; it need not be expensive or special, but it should be palatable.

Glossary

BAKE BLIND
To prepare a tart case for filling–either because the filling is not cooked or it is very moist and will not allow the dough to bake properly–the raw pastry is prebaked. To prevent the dough from rising, it may be necessary to line it with parchment or waxed paper and fill it with pie weights or dry beans. The dough is then baked until ready to eat in the case of an uncooked filling, or until almost done if it is going to be filled and returned to the oven.

BARD
Bard refers to the thin strips of pork or bacon fat placed round meat, game, and poultry to protect the flesh from drying out when cooked in the oven. The strips of bard are held in place with kitchen twine. To bard is to surround the piece to be cooked with strips of fat.

BASTE
Food roasting in the oven is basted to moisten it so that it does not dry out. To baste, spoon over the cooking juices from the pan or brush the roast with them, and repeat several times during the cooking process.

BEAT
When the term "beat" is used, either a wire whisk or electric mixer may be used, unless a specific utensil is mentioned. The term is used most often in connection with egg whites, which are usually beaten until firm or stiff (*see* Beating Egg Whites).

BEATING EGG WHITES
Beating or whisking egg whites involves beating with a whisk or electric mixer until they stiffen and form soft or firm peaks, depending on what the recipe calls for. If firm peaks are required, the whites should be beaten until they peak and do not slide out of the mixing bowl when the bowl is turned upside down. Stiffly beaten egg whites are folded, not stirred, into other ingredients (*see* Fold); they must be used immediately after being beaten or they will separate and become watery.

BEURRE MANIÉ *see* Thickening or Enriching

BLANC (TO COOK IN)
Some vegetables that discolor during cooking, such as artichoke hearts, and white offal should be cooked in a *blanc*–water to which a little flour and lemon juice or vinegar are added.

BLANCH
To blanch a food is to cook it very briefly in boiling water, either to soften it before cooking or remove its bitterness. The food is then refreshed, either by being dipped rapidly in cold or ice water, or held under cold running water, and then drained.

BOUQUET GARNI
Unless otherwise specified in particular recipes, the usual components of a bouquet garni are some leek greens, a piece of celery stick, preferably with its leaves, a sprig of thyme, and a bay leaf.

BRAISE
Braising is a slow cooking method that uses a little liquid to gently simmer the meat, vegetables, or even fish, either in the oven or on the stovetop. A variant of braising, known as *cuire à l'étouffée*, requires sealing the pot, usually with a flour-and-water paste, so that no steam escapes.

BROWN OR COLOR
These two terms are used interchangeably. They generally refer to cooking a food in fat until the surface takes on a golden or brownish color. Instructions can vary, depending on the degree of color to be attained ("until it begins to color," "until lightly browned," or simply "brown").

Food should be browned in a pan large enough for it to all sit on the bottom without piling up; if this is impossible, the food will have to be browned in several batches. Browning is a preliminary operation, so even if the food is divided into batches to brown, it should all be placed in the pot together to finish cooking.

These terms can also be used in connection with roasting and baking; the meaning is the same, referring to the color the surface should attain.

CAUL
Caul, or caul fat, is the membrane laced with fat that surrounds the stomach of animals. Pig's caul in particular is often used to hold together ingredients that might come apart during cooking, such as *paupiettes* (thin slices of meat filled with stuffing) and stuffed cabbage leaves.

CLARIFY
To clarify a liquid is to ensure that it is clear by removing any impurities. This is usually done with careful skimming as it simmers. When it cools, strain it through a fine-mesh sieve or cheesecloth.

To clarify butter, melt it slowly until most of its water content evaporates. The milk solids will sink to the bottom and gold-colored liquid will remain at the top. Skim off the foam and use the clear butter for your cooking.

COAT
To cover a dish smoothly with a sauce or a cream preparation. A sauce or cream preparation is ready when it coats the back of a spoon.

COLOR *see* Brown or Color

CRÈME FRAÎCHE
Crème fraîche is a very thick, rich cream that is frequently used in French cuisine. In most cases–and this is indicated in the recipes concerned–heavy cream can be used instead, but try to use crème fraîche if possible. It is now commercialized on a small scale in the US.

DEGLAZE

To deglaze means to pour liquid (usually wine or another alcoholic beverage, or stock) into a pan at high temperature so that the juices and sediments can be absorbed to make a sauce.

DEGREASING (REMOVING FAT)

For a stock or the broth of a pot-au-feu, removing the fat requires skimming it off with a small ladle as it rises while the liquid simmers. An easier method is to leave the liquid to chill until the fat hardens at the surface, at which stage it is easily removed with a slotted spoon or even an ordinary spoon. If you are in a hurry, use paper towel to absorb fat from the surface.

DEMI-GLACE (Demi-Glaze) see *Glace* and *Demi-Glace* (Glaze and Demi-Glaze)

DICE

Many recipes call for diced vegetables, aromatics, and other ingredients. The sizes required vary. A **brunoise** is made of extremely fine dice, cubes of approximately $\frac{1}{12}$ in. (2-3 mm). A **salpicon** requires slightly larger dice, approximately ¼-in. (5-mm) cubes. For a **mirepoix**, the size ranges from ¼-½ in. (5-10 mm), depending on whether it is prepared for a sauce or a stock. By dicing all the ingredients to the same size, you will ensure that they cook more evenly. If used as a garnish, they will be all the more attractive.

DOUBLE BOILER

A double boiler is a pan that consists of two parts: a bottom, in which a little water is placed and brought just below the boiling point to simmer, and a top, in which the ingredients to be cooked over the simmering water are placed. It is important that the water should simmer, not boil, and that it should never touch the bottom of the top section. A double boiler can be improvised by heating water in a saucepan and setting a mixing bowl (preferably stainless steel) over it (make sure the bottom of the bowl does not touch the water).

DUTCH OVEN

Known as a *cocotte* in French, this is a large pot with a tight-fitting lid, ideal for stews as it can be used both on the stove top and in the oven. It is usually made of cast iron.

ENRICHING see Thickening or Enriching

FLAMBÉ

To pour an alcoholic beverage, often cognac or other liqueur, over a dish and then set light to it. This will intensify the flavor, particularly when the pan juices are required in a sauce.

To flambé desserts, warm the liqueur a little in a deep dish, pour it over the hot food, ignite it using a long match set at the edge of the dish, and allow the flames to burn out.

FOUR-SPICE MIX

Classic French cuisine uses few spices, but makes frequent use of this blend of ground black pepper, nutmeg, ginger, and cloves.

GLACE AND DEMI-GLACE (GLAZE AND DEMI-GLAZE)

A *glace* is a reduction of a tasty, gelatinous meat stock to about one tenth of its volume. A *demi-glace* is made by thickening a stock with a roux (butter and flour cooked together) and then reducing it, but by less than for a *glace*. Commercial preparations are available as a substitute for these ingredients.

GRATIN

A gratin is a dish with a topping such as bread crumbs or cheese that is placed under the broiler until crisp and browned.

GRILL PAN

Available in square, rectangular, and round forms, this is a heavy pan usually used for high-heat cooking of meat, and sometimes vegetables. It allows individual portions of meat, such as steaks, to be grilled and seared in attractive crisscross patterns, and ensures that they do not cook in their own fat.

JULIENNE STRIPS

These are very thin strips of about 2 in. (5 cm) in length. The easiest way to make them is to cut the vegetable into 2-in. (5-cm) lengths, then into slices about $\frac{1}{16}$ in. (2 mm) thick. Pile the slices up two or three at a time, and cut them into strips $\frac{1}{16}$ in. (2 mm) wide.

JUS

In the recipes here, *jus* refers to the leftover cooking juices from a roast, preferably a veal roast. Since it is not always practical to store this, commercially made preparations of *jus* or reduced stock are a good substitute.

PURÉE

To crush or blend to a cream or paste, generally in a blender, but a food processor or food mill will often work as well.

Starchy vegetables (potatoes, split peas, etc.) should never be puréed in a blender or food processor: use a food mill, potato ricer or masher, or wire whisk.

REDUCE

To boil or simmer a preparation until it reduces in volume and thickens.

REFRESH

To refresh means to cool down rapidly. Vegetables are refreshed to stop the cooking process thereby retaining their texture and color, by placing them briefly under running water and draining. Pasta is also refreshed to preserve its texture. Sauces and creams are refreshed by placing them in a bowl set over a larger bowl of cold water and ice.

SCALE

To remove the scales of a fish by scraping the skin from the tail toward the head. This should be done carefully so the skin is not damaged.

SIMMER

To cook gently over low heat, as opposed to boiling.

SKIM

To remove the impurities that rise to the surface during the slow boiling of a stock or sauce and that form a filmy layer. This is usually done using a skimmer (large spoon-shaped utensil with fine holes).

STOCK POT

This is a high-sided pot that ensures slow evaporation, making it perfect for preparing stocks or soups.

SWEAT

To cook vegetables, aromatic ingredients, and sometimes fruit very briefly so that they do not change color and merely soften, exuding their own liquid. Onions and shallots should become translucent.

THICKENING OR ENRICHING

To thicken a preparation (usually a sauce), add either egg yolk, butter, beurre manié, flour, or other starch to give it more consistency.

If you are using egg yolks to thicken a hot liquid, begin by pouring a little of the hot liquid into the yolks and mixing well. This will heat the yolks somewhat and prevent them from coagulating when they come into contact with the hot substance.

Butter should be unsalted and well chilled: dice it and whisk it in gradually until you have the right consistency; do not allow it to boil for any more than a couple of seconds, otherwise the butter will separate.

To use flour or another starch such as cornstarch, first dilute it in a little liquid to make a thin paste (leave no lumps) and then add it to the preparation that requires thickening. Stir as you heat until it comes to a boil and thickens.

A **roux** is the first stage in a sauce and is made of flour cooked with butter, to which liquid is gradually added. Recipes may call for a roux of a darker color than white; in this case, cook the butter and flour until it reaches the desired color.

Beurre manié is prepared by making a paste of equal quantities of butter and flour. Soften the butter and cream it into the flour using a fork until you have a smooth paste. Beurre manié is used as a thickening agent.

Some traditional dishes, like coq au vin, require blood as a thickening agent.

TRIM

To remove the pieces of fat, sinew, and other inedible parts from meat (and other foods) that would otherwise detract from the shape and texture. Trimmings may be used to make stock. Vegetables may be trimmed to improve their appearance.

TRUSS

To truss is to thread fine twine through the body of a poultry or game bird to keep the legs and wings in place as it cooks. A roast may also be trussed to facilitate the cooking process.

ZEST

This is the thin, colored, outer layer of citrus fruit peels. It can either be removed in strips with a vegetable peeler or grated off with a fine-holed grater, depending on how it is being used. When zest is called for, first wash off the fruit in warm water and wipe it dry. If grating the zest, be careful to grate off only the colored part of the peel; the white, spongy part of the peel, just under the zest, has a very strong, bitter taste. Whenever possible, use fruits that have not been sprayed with chemicals.

Index

Page numbers in *italics*
refer to recipe illustrations

Notes